RAF

DEFENCE

APTITUDE

ASSESSMENT

As part of this product you have also received **FREE** access to online tests that will help you to pass the RAF selection tests:

To gain access, simply go to:

www.MyPsychometricTests.com

Get more products for passing any test at:

www.How2Become.com

Orders: Please contact www.How2Become.com

You can order through Amazon.co.uk under ISBN: **9781912370931**, via the website www.How2Become.com or through Gardners.com.

ISBN: **9781912370931**

First published in 2022 by How2Become Ltd..

Copyright © 2022 How2Become.

All rights reserved. Apart from any permitted use under UK copyright law, no part of this publication may be reproduced or transmitted in any form or by any means, electronic or mechanical, including photocopying, recording, or any information, storage or retrieval system, without permission in writing from the publisher or under licence from the Copyright Licensing Agency Limited. Further details of such licenses (for reprographic reproduction) may be obtained from the Copyright Licensing Agency Ltd, Saffron House, 6-10 Kirby Street, London EC1N 8TS.

Typeset by Andrew Bosworth for How2Become Ltd.

Disclaimer

Every effort has been made to ensure that the information contained within this guide is accurate at the time of publication. How2Become Ltd is not responsible for anyone failing any part of any selection process as a result of the information contained within this guide. How2Become Ltd and their authors cannot accept any responsibility for any errors or omissions within this guide, however caused. No responsibility for loss or damage occasioned by any person acting, or refraining from action, as a result of the material in this publication can be accepted by How2Become Ltd.

The information within this guide does not represent the views of any third party service or organisation.

CONTENTS

INTRODUCTION	7
PREFACE BY AUTHOR RICHARD MCMUNN	11
CHAPTER 1 About the RAF DAA	13
CHAPTER 2 Tips for Passing the RAF DAA	17
CHAPTER 3 The Verbal Reasoning Test	21
CHAPTER 4 The Numerical Reasoning Test	49
CHAPTER 5 The Spatial Reasoning Test	75
CHAPTER 6 The Work Rate Test	101
CHAPTER 7 The Mechanical Comprehension Test	117

CHAPTER 8
The Electrical Comprehension Test

INTRODUCTION

Welcome to your new guide, *RAF Defence Aptitude Assessment: Sample Test Questions* for the Royal Air Force. This guide was written with the rigorous selection process of the Royal Air Force in mind.

Here at How2Become, we know how complex the RAF selection tests can be. As the UK's leading career and testing specialists, it is our aim to put together a testing guide that will assist you during your preparation.

The selection tests for the RAF are designed to assess potential employees' 'suitability' for specific job posts. When you apply to join the RAF as an airman or airwoman, you will undergo a challenging selection test, the DAA formerly known as the Airman/Airwoman Selection Test).

With the help of this guide, you will be able to prepare for the types of question you are to face during your RAF selection test. This guide is packed full of testing questions to give you some idea of what you can expect in terms of question type and the skills required.

We have created an easy-to-follow guide that breaks up the selection process into small, manageable sections.

Below we have outlined the contents of this guide:

1. Verbal Reasoning;
2. Numerical Reasoning;
3. Spatial Reasoning;
4. Work Rate;
5. Mechanical Comprehension;
6. Electrical Comprehension;

For best results, we recommend that you work through the guide in the order that it is written. However, if you would like to focus on one particular test, use the contents to locate which test you want to begin.

If you want more information about preparing for life in the RAF, then here at How2Become, we offer a wide range of products to assist you at www.How2Become.com.

Good luck and best wishes,

The How2Become Team

PREFACE BY AUTHOR RICHARD MCMUNN

Before you get your head into the game, and start practising for your RAF Defence Aptitude Assessment, I thought it might be a good idea to introduce myself; explaining my background, and why I'm qualified to help you pass the selection process for joining the RAF.

At the time of writing, I am 50 years old and living in Tunbridge Wells, Kent. I left school at the usual age of 16 and joined the Royal Navy, serving on-board HMS Invincible as part of 800 Naval Air Squadron which formed part of the Fleet Air Arm. There I was, at the age of 16, travelling the world and working as an engineer on Sea Harrier jets! It was fantastic and I loved every minute of it!

After four years, I left the Royal Navy and joined Kent Fire and Rescue Service as a firefighter. Over the next 17 years, I worked my way up through the ranks to the position of Assistant Divisional Officer. During my time in the fire service, I spent a lot of time working as an instructor at the Fire Brigade Training Centre. I was also involved in the selection process for assessing candidates who wanted to become firefighters. Therefore, my knowledge and experience gained so far in life has been invaluable in helping people like you to pass any type of selection process. I am sure you will find this guide an invaluable resource during your preparation for joining the Royal Air Force.

I have always been fortunate in the fact that I persevere in everything I set my mind to. I understand that if I keep working hard in life, then I will always be successful, or at least know that I have done my very best! This is an important lesson that I want you to take on board.

If you work hard and persevere, then success will come your way. The same rule applies when applying for a career in the Armed Forces; if you work hard and make the most out of your preparation time, then you will be successful.

Finally, it is very important that you believe in your own abilities. It does not matter if you have no qualifications; it does not matter if you are currently weak in the area of psychometric testing. What does matter is self-belief, self-discipline, and a genuine desire to improve and become successful.

Best wishes,

Richard McMunn

CHAPTER 1 – ABOUT THE RAF DAA

RAF DEFENCE APTITUDE ASSESSMENT

Before we get into some sample practice questions for the Royal Air Force Selection Test (DAA), let's first recap on what the test actually involves.

The DAA consists of a number of different aptitude tests, which are designed to assess which careers in the RAF you are most suited to. There are many different career opportunities available, and each one requires a different level of skill.

The DAA consists of sIx timed multiple-choice aptitude tests. These are as follows:

VERBAL REASONING	• This assessment is used to assess candidates' ability to interpret written information. • In the real assessment, you will be given 15 minutes to answer 20 questions.
NUMERICAL REASONING	• This assessment is used to assess mathematical knowledge, including arithmetics and data interpretation. • In the real assessment, the test is split into two sections. In the first section, you will be given 4 minutes to answer 12 questions. In the second section, you will be given 11 minutes to answer 15 questions.
SPATIAL REASONING	• This test assesses candidates' ability to work with shapes and 3D objects. • In the real assessment, you will be given 4 minutes to answer 10 questions.
WORK RATE	• This assessment is an aptitude test which assess candidates' ability to work through routine rasks as quickly and effectively as possible. • In the real assessment, you will be given 4 minutes to answer 20 questions.

MECHANICAL COMPREHENSION	• This assessment is an aptitude test which focusses on mechanical concepts. • In the real assessment, you will be given 10 minutes to answer 20 questions.
ELECTRICAL COMPREHENSION	• This assessment is an aptitude test which focusses on electrical concepts. • In the real assessment, you will be given 11 minutes to answer 21 questions.

Now that you understand what the test will involve, let's move on to some tips. These tips will help you to make the most out of your preparation time.

Read through the tips before attempting the sample tests.

CHAPTER 2 – TIPS TO PREPARE YOU FOR THE RAF DAA

There's no two ways about it, the most effective way in which you can prepare for your assessment, is to carry out lots of sample test questions. When we say lots, we mean lots!

Before we provide you with an array of test questions, here are a few important tips for you to consider:

- It is important that before you sit the RAF assessment, you find out as much information about the nature of the test. Most importantly, you need to find out the type(s) of questions that are going to appear. You should also take steps to find out if the tests will be timed, and also whether or not they will be of a multiple-choice format. By finding out this information prior to your assessment, that means you can tailor your sample tests to mimic the actual nature of the real assessment.

- Variety is the key to success. We recommend that you attempt a variety of different test questions, such as numerical reasoning, verbal reasoning, fault analysis, spatial reasoning and mechanical reasoning. This will undoubtedly improve your overall ability to pass the test. For more help on the aforementioned tests, please check out the following resources on www.How2Become.com.

CHAPTER 2 – TIPS TO PREPARE YOU FOR THE RAF DAA

- Confidence is an important part of preparation. How many times have you sat a test or exam, and your mind goes blank? This happens to the majority of us. This is because you are nervous, stressed and focussing on the negatives. Instead, you need to try to put yourself in a positive mindset. If your confidence is at its peak, then there is no doubt that your test scores will greatly improve.

- Whilst this is a very basic tip that may appear obvious, many people neglect to follow it. Make sure that you get a good sleep the night before your RAF Defence Aptitude Assessment. Research has shown that those people who have regular 'good' sleep are far more likely to demonstrate higher concentration levels during psychometric tests.

- Try practising numerical test questions in your head, without writing down your calculations. This is very difficult to accomplish, but it is excellent practice for the real test. Also, practise numerical reasoning tests without a calculator. If you are permitted to use a calculator at the test, make sure you know how to use one!

- You are what you eat! In the week prior to the test, eat and drink healthily. Avoid cigarettes, alcohol and food with high fat content. The reason for this is that these will make you feel sluggish and you will not perform to your best ability on the day. On the morning of your assessment, eat a healthy breakfast such as porridge and a banana.

- ALWAYS drink plenty of water.

- If you have any special needs that need to be catered for, ensure you inform the assessment centre staff PRIOR to the assessment day. By doing so, they will be able to provide you with additional support (such as extra time). This can only work to your advantage, so be sure to let them know of any learning difficulty or other needs.

Now that we have provided you with a number of important tips, take the time to work through the many different sample test questions that are contained within the guide.

In order to complete the tests accurately, use a stopwatch to time yourself for each section.

RAF DEFENCE APTITUDE ASSESSMENT

Please note that the tests used in this book are to be used as a GUIDELINE only. Whilst we have tried our best to provide similar tests to the real thing, we cannot guarantee exact exam-style questions.

However, these sample tests are a great way to increase the key skills required for each section of the asessment.

CHAPTER 3 — VERBAL REASONING TESTS

During the Royal Air Force Defence Aptitude Assessment, you will be required to sit a Verbal Reasoning Test.

Verbal Reasoning is the ability to analyse and comprehend information. The RAF selection process uses this form of aptitude test as a way of measuring candidates' ability to read through information and 'pick out' key information.

Preparing for verbal reasoning assessments can be tricky, but we believe that the best way to prepare, is to have a go at similar verbal reasoning assessments.

During the actual Verbal Reasoning Test with the RAF, you will have a specific amount of time to answer each question. Read through each extract carefully and answer the questions that follow.

In the real test, there are 20 questions you need to answer. You will be given 20 minutes to complete this assessment.

CHAPTER 3 – VERBAL REASONING TESTS

VERBAL REASONING PRACTICE QUESTION

> Barry and Bill work at their local supermarket in the town of Whiteham. Barry works every day, except Wednesday. The supermarket is run by Barry's brother, Elliot, who is married to Sarah.
>
> Sarah and Elliot have 2 children, Marcus and Michelle, who are both 7 years old, and they live in the road adjacent to the supermarket.
>
> Barry lives in a town called Redford, which is 7 miles from Whiteham.
>
> Bill's girlfriend Maria works in a factory in her hometown of Brownhaven.
>
> Sarah and Elliot take their children on holiday to Tenford twice a year and Barry usually gives them a lift in his car.
>
> The town of Redford is 6 miles from the seaside town of Tenford.
>
> Barry's mum lives in Tenford and he tries to visit her once a week, at 2pm, when he has a day off work.

Question 1

Which town does Elliot live in?

A. Redford

B. Whiteham

C. Brownhaven

D. Tenford

E. Cannot say

How to answer the question:

When it comes to questions like this, it involves a simple process of elimination.

In the second paragraph, we are told that Sarah and Elliot live adjacent to the supermarket. In the first paragraph, we are told that the supermarket can be located in the town of Whiteham.

Therefore, Elliot must also live in Whiteham.

Question 2

On which day of the week does Barry visit his mother?

A. Cannot say

B. Monday

C. Tuesday

D. Wednesday

E. Thursday

How to answer the question:

Again, it's all about the process of elimination.

In the first paragraph, we are told that Barry works every day except for Wednesdays. In the last paragraph, we are told that Barry visits his mother once a week on a day he is not working.

We know, from reading the first paragraph, that Barry doesn't work Wednesday, so this is the day he would be able to go and visit his mother.

Question 3

Bill and Maria live together in Brownhaven.

A. True

B. False

C. Cannot say

How to answer the question:

From reading the passage, it is not made clear as to whether or not Bill and Maria live together.

Although the passage tells us that Maria works in Brownhaven, it is not made clear as to a) whether she lives there, and b) whether or not Bill lives with her.

CHAPTER 3 – VERBAL REASONING TESTS

Therefore, the answer is C: cannot say.

Now that we've looked at a sample verbal reasoning question, have a go at the following practice test.

VERBAL REASONING EXERCISE 1

Read the following information carefully before answering the questions that follow. You have 5 minutes to complete exercise 1.

> **FLAT A** is located in a town. It is 12 miles from the nearest train station. It has 2 bedrooms and is located on the ground floor. The monthly rental is £450 and the council tax is £50 per month. The lease is for 6 months.
>
> **FLAT B** is located in the city centre and is 2 miles from the nearest train station. It is located on the 3rd floor. The monthly rental is £600 and the council tax is £130 per month. The lease is for 6 months and it has 3 bedrooms.
>
> **FLAT C** is located in the city centre and is 3 miles from the nearest train station. It is located on the 1st floor and has 1 bedroom. The monthly rental is £550 and the council tax is £100 per month. The lease is for 12 months.
>
> **FLAT D** is located in a town. The monthly rental is £395 per month and the council tax is £100 per month. It is located on the ground floor and the lease is for 6 months. It is 18 miles from the nearest train station. The flat has 2 bedrooms.
>
> **FLAT E** is located in a village and is 12 miles from the nearest train station. It has 3 bedrooms and is located on the 2nd floor. The monthly rental is £375 and the council tax is £62. It has a lease of 12 months.

Question 1

You want a flat that is within 10 miles of the nearest train station, and is located on the 1st floor or lower. The combined monthly rent and council tax bill must be no greater than £600. Which flat would you choose?

A. Flat A

B. Flat B

C. Flat C

D. Flat D

E. None of the above

Question 2

You want a flat that has at least 2 bedrooms and has a combined monthly rent and tax bill that does not exceed £450. Which flat would you choose?

A. Flat A

B. Flat B

C. Flat C

D. Flat D

E. Flat E

Question 3

You want a flat that has a combined monthly rent and council tax bill that is not in excess to £700. It needs to be within 15 miles of the train station, and have a lease for 6 months. Which flat would you choose?

A. Flat A

B. Flat B

C. Flat C

D. Flat D

E. Flat E

VERBAL REASONING EXERCISE 2

Read the following information carefully before answering the questions that follow.

You have 5 minutes to complete exercise 2.

> Cardiovascular disease is so prevalent that virtually all businesses are likely to have employees who suffer from, or may develop, this condition.
>
> Research shows that between 51-80% of all people who suffer a heart attack, are able to return to work. However, this may not be possible if they have previously been involved in heavy physical work.
>
> In such cases, it may be possible to move the employee to lighter duties, with appropriate retraining where necessary.
>
> Similarly, high-pressure, stressful work, even where it does not involve physical activity, should also be avoided.
>
> Human Resources managers should be aware of the implications of job roles for employees with a cardiac condition.

Question 1

Physical or stressful work may bring on a heart attack.

A. True

B. False

C. Cannot say

Question 2

The majority of people who have suffered a heart attack can later return to work.

A. True

B. False

C. Cannot say

Question 3

Heart disease may affect enmployees in any type of business.

A. True

B. False

C. Cannot say

VERBAL REASONING EXERCISE 3

Read the following information carefully before answering the questions that follow.

You have 5 minutes to complete exercise 3.

> Although there is not a clear cause for abdominal pain in children, it may be a symptom of emotional disturbance, especially where it appears in conjunction with phobias or sleep disorders such as nightmares or sleep-walking.
>
> It may also be linked to eating habits: a study carried out in the USA found that children with pain tended to be fussier about what and how much they ate, and to have over-anxious parents who spent a considerable amount of time trying to persuade them to eat.
>
> Although abdominal pain had previously been linked to excessive milk-drinking, this research found that children with pain drank rather less milk than those in the control group.

CHAPTER 3 – VERBAL REASONING TESTS

Question 1

There is no clear cause for abdominal pain in children.

A. True

B. False

C. Cannot say

Question 2

Abdominal pain in children is caused by eating too much.

A. True

B. False

C. Cannot say

Question 3

Drinking milk may help to prevent abdominal pain in children.

A. True

B. False

C. Cannot say

VERBAL REASONING EXERCISE 4

Read the following information carefully before answering the questions that follow.

You have 5 minutes to complete exercise 4.

> Jeff Roberts claims he has had his garden shed broken into. A crowbar was found in the garden and the door of the shed had been forced open. Mr Roberts claims that a lawn mower, a strimmer, a new spade and a garden fork have been stolen.
>
> He says that last week a group of young people graffitied the side wall of his house and he thinks they are to blame.
>
> The ringleader of the gang, Sam Smith, has recently started a gardening company.
>
> The latest reported facts are:
>
> - Sam Smith has previous convictions for breaking and entering.
> - Sam Smith has a variety of new gardening equipment for his company – including a spade the same as Mr Roberts.
> - Mr Roberts' spade was bought from popular high street shop.
> - Mr Roberts stolen items are worth £400.
> - Mr Roberts says Sam Smith has been harassing him.
> - Sam Smith's dad fired Mr Roberts from his marketing company last month.

Question 1

Mr Roberts has a grudge against Sam Smith.

A. True

B. False

C. Cannot say

Question 2

The items stolen from Mr Roberts' shed are worth more than £400.

A. True

B. False

C. Cannot say

Question 3

Sam Smith may have stolen Mr Roberts' spade.

A. True

B. False

C. Cannot say

VERBAL REASONING EXERCISE 5

Read the following information carefully before answering the questions that follow.

You have 5 minutes to complete exercise 5.

> Below is a company ordering process.
>
> 1.1 Our display of products and online services on our website are an invitation and not an offer to sell those goods to you.
>
> 1.2 An offer is made when you place the order for your products or online service. However, we will not have made a contract with you unless and until we accept your offer.
>
> 1.3 We take payment from your card when we process your order and have checked your card details. Goods are subject to availability. If we are unable to supply the goods, we will inform you of this as soon as possible. A full refund will be given if you hae already paid for the goods. It is our aim to always keep our website updted and all goods displayed are available.
>
> 1.4 If you enter a correct email address, we will send you an order acknowledgement email immediately, along with a receipt of payment. These do not constitute an order confirmation or order acceptance from us.
>
> 1.5 Unless we have notified you that we do not accept your order or you have cancelled it, order acceptance and the creation of the contract between you and us will take place at the point the goods have ordered are dispatched from our premises.
>
> 1.6 The contract will be formed at the place of dispatch of the goods. All goods, wherever possible, will be dispatched within 24 hours of the order being placed, Monday to Thursday. If your order falls on a weekend or bank holiday, your order will be dispatched on the next available working day. All orders are sent recorded delivery, and will require a signature. In the majority of cases, however, we will dispatch goods using Royal Mail's standard First Class delivery service.

CHAPTER 3 – VERBAL REASONING TESTS

Question 1

If a customer places an order, and they have entered a correct email address, they will immediately receive an order confirmation email.

A. True

B. False

C. Cannot say

Question 2

Orders placed on a Friday will be dispatched on a Saturday.

A. True

B. False

C. Cannot say

Question 3

Payment is taken from the card once the card details have been checked.

A. True

B. False

C. Cannot say

VERBAL REASONING EXERCISE 6

Read the following information carefully before answering the questions that follow.

You have 5 minutes to complete exercise 6.

> The Special Air Service was originally founded by Lieutenant David Stirling during World War II. The initial purpose of the regiment was to be a long-range desert patrol group required to conduct raids and sabotage operations far behind the enemy lines.
>
> Lieutenant Stirling was a member of Number 8 Commando Regiment and he specifically looked for recruits who were both talented and individual specialists in their field. He looked for initiative.
>
> The first mission of the SAS turned out to be a disaster. They were operating in support of Field Marshal Calude Auchinleck's attack in November 1941, but only 22 out of 62 SAS troopers deployed reached the rendezvous point. However, Stirling still managed to organise another attack against the German airfields at Aqedabia, Site of Agheila, which successfully destroyed 61 enemy aircraft, without a single casualty. After that, the 1st SAS earned regimental status and Stirling's brother, Bill, began to arrange a second regiment called Number 2 SAS.
>
> It was during the desert war that they performed a number of successful insertion missions and destroyed many aircraft and fuel depots in the process. Their success contributed towards Hitler issuing his Kommandobefehl order to execute all captured Commandos. The Germans then stepped up security and as a result, the SAS changed their tactics. They used jeeps armed with Vickers K machine guns and used tracer ammunition to ignite fuel and aircraft. When the Italians captured David Stirling, he was sent to Colditz Castle and was held as a prisoner of war for the remainder of World War II. His brother, Bill, and 'Paddy' Blair Mayne, then took command of the regiment.

CHAPTER 3 – VERBAL REASONING TESTS

Question 1

During the SAS's first mission, only 42 of the total troopers deployed reached the rendezvous point.

A. True

B. False

C. Cannot say

Question 2

When the Germans captured David Stirling, he ended up in Colditz Castle as a prisoner for the remainder of the war.

A. True

B. False

C. Cannot say

Question 3

Lieutenant Stirling was member of Number 8 SAS Regiment.

A. True

B. False

C. Cannot say

VERBAL REASONING EXERCISE 7

Read the following information carefully before answering the questions that follow.

You have 5 minutes to complete exercise 7.

> Brendon and his youngest brother, Jason, live in the middle of Maidstone. It is a short walking distance from their house to the supermarket. Every morning, they walk the same route and part at the supermarket, which is where Brendon works. Jason continues his journey with his friend, Pete. Every morning, they make their way to Linton College, a 2-minute walk from the supermarket.
>
> Madeline lives in a small village on the outskirts of the town where she used to live. Her sister, Rachel, attends a grammar school in Tunbridge Wells. She travels from her house in Marden via train, to get to school each day. Most days, Rachel sits next to her friend Matt on the train.
>
> Matt gets on the train in his home town of Staplehurst. When Matt doesn't get the train, he drives his sister's car. His sister is called Polly and she too, works at the same supermarket as Brendon.

CHAPTER 3 – VERBAL REASONING TESTS

Question 1

Where does Polly work?

A. Staplehurst

B. Marden

C. Maidstone

D. Tunbridge Wells

Question 2

Where does Rachel go to school?

A. Staplehurst

B. Marden

C. Maidstone

D. Tunbridge Wells

Question 3

Which of the following is definitely true?

A. Brendon is older than Jason.

B. Jason is older than Pete.

C. Brendon is older than Polly.

D. Madeline is older than Rachel.

VERBAL REASONING EXERCISE 8

Read the following information carefully before answering the questions that follow.

You have 5 minutes to complete exercise 8.

> Under the Race Relations (Amendment) Act, public authorities (including the Fire and Rescue Service) have a general duty to promote race equality. This means that when carrying out their functions or duties, they must have due regard to the need to:
>
> - Eliminate discrimination;
> - Promote equality of opportunity;
> - Promote good relations between persons of different racial groups.
>
> In order to demonstrate how Fire and Rescue Service plan to meet their statutory duties, they have an obligation to produce and publish what is called a Race Equality Scheme. The Race Equality Scheme outlines their strategy and action plan to ensure that equality and diversity are mainstreamed through their policies, practices, procedures and functions. Central to this strategy are external consultation, monitoring and assessment, training, and ensuring that the public have access to this information.
>
> *"Equality is not about treating everybody the same, but recognising we are all individuals, unique in our own way. Equality and fairness is about recognising, accepting and valuing people's unique individuality according to their needs. This often means that individuals may be treated appropriately, yet fairly, based on their needs."*

Question 1

Any form of racism is unwelcome in the Fire Service.

A. True

B. False

C. Cannot say

Question 2

The general public does have access to the Race Equality Scheme.

A. True

B. False

C. Cannot say

Question 3

The Fire Service may promote good relations between persons of different racial groups.

A. True

B. False

C. Cannot say

VERBAL REASONING EXERCISE 9

Read the following information carefully before answering the questions that follow.

You have 5 minutes to complete exercise 9.

> The summers in Australia can bring total devastation to many through the many bushfires which occur. Bushfires destroy livelihoods, property, machinery, eucalyptus forests and they can even spread to the suburban areas of major cities.
>
> Although all bushfires can have a devastating effect, few of them fall under the 'disaster' category. Some of these falling into this category are:
>
> - Victoria (2009): 173 lives were lost in this bushfire, so it is more commonly referred to as Black Saturday;
> - South Australia and Victoria (1983): This claimed 76 lives and was named as Ash Wednesday;
> - Southern Victoria (1969): 23 lives were claimed;
> - New South Wales (1968): There were 14 fatalities in this bushfire in the Blue Mountains and coastal region;
> - Hobart and Southern Tasmania (1967): 62 people were killed;
> - Victoria (1939): This was named Black Friday after 71 people lost their lives.
>
> There are two different types of bushfire in Australia – grass fires and forest fires. Grass fires more commonly occur on grazing and farm land. These often destroy fences, livestock, machinery, and sometimes human lives. Forest fires are largely made up of eucalyptus trees. These are extremely difficult to control due to the high amounts of flammable vapour from the leaves. The bushfires are fought by large numbers of trained volunteer firefighters. Helicopters and light aircraft are sometimes used to make observations about the fire and some also have the capacity to carry water. Aircraft used to carry water in order to extinguish forest fires often find that the visibility is extremely poor, preventing them from getting close enough to the fire in order to extinguish it with their quantities of water.

CHAPTER 3 – VERBAL REASONING TESTS

Question 1

Aircraft deployed to extinguish bushfires struggle to get close to the fire due to the heat.

A. True

B. False

C. Cannot say

Question 2

In total, there have been 419 fatalities from Australian bushfires since 1939.

A. True

B. False

C. Cannot say

Question 3

Hundreds of animals are killed by bushfires each year.

A. True

B. False

C. Cannot say

VERBAL REASONING EXERCISE 10

Read the following information carefully before answering the questions that follow.

You have 5 minutes to complete exercise 10.

> There are two separate options offered for account billing:
>
> Monthly: This option operates on a 4-week cycle beginning on the day of account activation.
>
> Annually: This option operates on a 365-day cycle beginning on the day of account activation.
>
> Note: Customers on a monthly billing cycle are beilled every 4 weeks.
>
> When your account reaches its appropriate billing day (your account's expiration date), your credit card will be automatically billed for the next billing cycle and your account expiration date will be extended by an additional 4 weeks (or 365 for annual packages). You will receive a receipt via email. If the transaction is unsuccessful for any reason, we will attempt to re-bill your credit card for 2 consecutive days and send an unsuccessful renewal email for each unsuccessful attempt (to your accounts specified Billing Profile email address).
>
> After your first unsuccessful renewal attempt, your account status will be updated to Billing Hold Level 1. This status indicates that your account is overdue but otherwise has no direct effect on your service which will continue for up to 4 weeks following your actual expiration date.
>
> 4 weeks after your account expires, we will attempt to re-bill your credit card for two monthly payments. If successful, your account expiration date will be extended by an additional 4 weeks (from bill date) and you will receive a receipt via email. If unsuccessful, your account status will be updated to Billing Hold Level 2. This status indicates that your account is now more than 4 weeks overdue and will close all ccount service until payment has been received. We will attempt to re-bill your credit card for 2 consecutive dats and send an unsuccessful renewal email for each unsuccessful attempt.
>
> When your account is in this status, you will still be able to log in and access both the Earn Cash page (to manage affiliate referrals and

the Renew Account page).

56 days after your account expires, we will attempt to re-bill your credit card for three monthly payments. If successful, your account expiration date will be extended by an additional 3 weeks (from bill date), your account will be reactivated and you will receive a receipt via email. If unsuccessful, your account will be permanently closed.

Question 1

Billing Hold Level 1 occurs after the first unsuccessful renewal attempt.

A. True

B. False

C. Cannot say

Question 2

Billing Hold Level 2 occurs when an attempt to take two monthly payments after an account is 4 weeks past account expiration fails.

A. True

B. False

C. Cannot say

Question 3

Customers who opt for the monthly billing option will be billed every 4 weeks on the first day of each month.

A. True

B. False

C. Cannot say

ANSWERS TO VERBAL REASONING TESTS

EXERCISE 1

1. E

2. E

3. A

EXERCISE 2

1. C

2. A

3. A

EXERCISE 3

1. A

2. C

3. C

EXERCISE 4

1. C

2. C

3. A

EXERCISE 5

1. B

2. B

3. A

EXERCISE 6

1. B

2. B

3. B

EXERCISE 7

1. C

2. D

3. A

EXERCISE 8

1. A

2. A

3. B

EXERCISE 9

1. B

2. C

3. C

EXERCISE 10

1. A

2. A

3. C

Now that you've completed sample questions for verbal reasoning, let's take a look at the next section – numerical reasoning.

CHAPTER 4 – NUMERICAL REASONING TESTS

RAF DEFENCE APTITUDE ASSESSMENT

During the RAF Defence Aptitude Assessmrent, you will be required to undertake a Numerical Reasoning Test. This test is used to determine how accurately you can interpret numerical information such as charts, graphs and tables. These will also assess your ability to use fractions, decimals and other basic arithmetic.

As you can imagine, the most effective way to prepare for this type of test is to carry out lots of sample numiercal reasoning test questions, without the aid of a calculator!

In the real test, you will have 4 minutes to complete 12 questions in part 1, and 11 minutes to complete 15 questions for part 2.

Before we begin, let's quickly take a look at some of the mathematical topics that you should revise BEFORE sitting your RAF numerical assessment.

Fractions	Decimals	Percentages
Values	Basic Arithmetic	Basic Algebra
Charts	Tables	Graphs

CHAPTER 4 – NUMERICAL REASONING TESTS

PART 1 OF NUMERICAL REASONING

You have 10 minutes to complete the 20 questions.

Question 1

Your friends tell you that their electricity bill has gone up from £40 per month to £47 per month. How much extra are they paying per year?

A	B	C	D	E
£84	£85	£83	£86	£82

Question 2

A woman earns a salary of £32,000 per year. How much would she earn in 15 years?

A	B	C	D	E
£280,000	£380,000	£480,000	£260,000	£460,000

Question 3

If a woman walks for 6 hours at a pace of 4km/h, how far will she have walked?

A	B	C	D	E
20km	21km	22km	23km	24km

Question 4

What is the value of x? $\dfrac{6x - 4}{2} = 19$

A	B	C	D	E
5	7	9	11	13

Question 5

Ellie spends 3 hours on the phone talking to her friend abroad. If the call costs 12 pence per 5 minutes, how much does the call cost?

A	B	C	D	E
£3.30	£4.32	£3.32	£4.44	£3.44

Question 6

A woman spends £27 in a retail store. She has a discount voucher that reduces the total cost from £27 to £21.60. What percentage was her discount voucher worth?

A	B	C	D	E
5%	10%	15%	20%	25%

Question 7

A group of 7 men spend £21.70 on a round of drinks. If the bill was split equally, how much would each person pay?

A	B	C	D	E
£3.00	£6.10	£3.10	£3.15	£3.20

Question 8

45,600 people attend a football match to watch Manchester United play Tottenham Hotspur. If there are 32,705 Manchester United supporters at the game, how many Tottenham Hotspur supporters are there?

A	B	C	D	E
12,985	13,985	12,890	12,895	14,985

CHAPTER 4 – NUMERICAL REASONING TESTS

Question 9

Calculate 5/7 − 2/3

A	B	C	D	E
2/3	1/21	1/11	3/21	3/4

Question 10

A car journey usually takes 6 hours and 55 minutes, but on one occasion the car stops for a total of 47 minutes. How long does the journey take on this occasion?

A	B	C	D	E
6 hours and 40 minutes	5 hours and 45 minutes	7 hours and 40 minutes	7 hours and 42 minutes	6 hours and 42 minutes

Question 11

There are 10 people in a team. Five of them weigh 70 kg each, and the remaining five weigh 75 kg each. Work out the average weight of the team.

A	B	C	D	E
72.5 kg	71.5 kg	70.5 kg	72 kg	71 kg

Question 12

Calculate 3.83 + 8.43

A	B	C	D	E
13.13	12.61	13.31	12.26	11.12

Question 13

What is ⅗ as a decimal?

A	B	C	D	E
0.60	0.30	0.25	0.40	0.35

Question 14

Using the rule of BIDMAS, work out 23.7 − 2.5 × 8.

A	B	C	D	E
169.6	3.7	4.8	196.6	130.6

Question 15

How many grams are there in 2.5 kilograms?

A	B	C	D	E
0.0025 g	250 g	2005 g	2,500 g	0.25 g

Question 16

Work out $\frac{4}{6} \times \frac{3}{5}$

A	B	C	D	E
12/25	12/40	6/20	2/5	1/5

Question 17

What is one quarter of 6 hours?

A	B	C	D	E
30 minutes	15 minutes	1 hour	1 hour and 30 minutes	2 hours and 15 minutes

Question 18

When paying a bill at the bank, you give the cashier one £20 note, two £5 notes, four £1 coins, six 10p coins, and two 2p coins. How much have you given the cashier?

A	B	C	D	E
£34.64	£43.46	£34.46	£63.44	£36.36

Question 19

If there are 610 metres in a mile, how many metres are there in 4 miles?

A	B	C	D	E
240	2,040	2,044	2,440	244

Question 20

A worker is required to work for 8 hours a day. He is entitled to three 20-minute breaks, and an hour for lunch during the working day. If he works for 5 days per week for 4 weeks, how many hours will he have actually worked?

A	B	C	D	E
12 hours	14 hours	120 hours	140 hours	150 hours

ANSWERS TO NUMERICAL REASONING TEST (PART 1)

Q1. a = £84

In this question you need to first work out the difference in their electricity bill. Subtract £40 from £47 to be left with £7. Now you need to calculate how much extra they are paying per year. If there are 12 months in a year then you need to multiply £7 by 12 months to reach your answer of £84.

Q2. c = £480,000

The lady earns £32,000 per year. To work out how much she earns in 15 years, you must multiply £32,000 by 15 years to reach your answer of £480,000.

Q3. e = 24km

To work this answer out all you need to do is multiply the 6 hours by the 4 km/h to reach the total of 24 km. Remember that she is walking at a pace of 4 km per hour for a total of 6 hours.

Q4. b = 7

To work out the value of x, you need to work backwards.

- 19 × 2 = 38
- 38 + 4 = 42
- 42 ÷ 6 = 7

To check that you have the correct answer, you can factor this back into the question, and see if it works.

CHAPTER 4 – NUMERICAL REASONING TESTS

Q5. b = £4.32

If the call costs 12 pence for every 5 minutes then all you need to do is calculate how many 5 minutes there are in the 3-hour telephone call. There are 60 minutes in every hour, so therefore there are 180 minutes in 3 hours. 180 minutes divided by 5 minutes will give you 36. To get your answer, just multiply 36 by 12 pence to reach your answer of £4.32

Q6. d = 20%

This type of question can be tricky, especially when you don't have a calculator! The best way to work out the answer is to first of all work out how much 10% discount would give you off the total price. If £27 is the total price, then 10% would be a £2.70 discount. In monetary terms the woman has received £5.40 in discount. If 10% is a £2.70 discount then 20% is a £5.40 discount.

Q7. c = £3.10

- Divide £21.70 by 7 to reach your answer of £3.10.

Q8. d = 12,895

- Subtract 32,705 from 45,600 to reach your answer of 12,895.

Q9. b = $1/21$

- 5 × 3 = 15
- 7 × 2 = 14
- 15 – 14 = 1
- 7 × 3 = 21
- This gives you the fraction of $1/21$.

Q10. d = 7 hrs 42 minutes

Add the 47 minutes to the normal journey time of 6 hrs and 55 minutes to reach your answer of 7 hrs and 42 minutes.

Q11. a = 72.5 kg

To calculate the average weight, you need to first of all add each weight together. Therefore, (5 × 70) + (5 × 75) = 725 kg. To find the average weight you must now divide the 725 by 10, which will give you the answer 72.5 kg.

Q12. d = 12.26

Q13. a = 0.60

To convert the fraction into a decimal you need to divide the top number by the bottom number (3 ÷ 5 = 0.6)

Q14. b = 3.7

This question asks you to use the method of BIDMAS:

- 2.5 × 8 = 20.

- 23.7 − 20 = 3.7

Q15. d = 2,500g

There are 1,000g in 1 kilogram. Therefore, 2,500g is equivalent to 2.5 kg (2.5 × 1,000 = 2,500g).

CHAPTER 4 – NUMERICAL REASONING TESTS

Q16. d = 2/5

- 4 × 3 = 12

- 5 × 6 = 30. So, 12/30 in its simplest form = 2/5

Q17. d = 1 hour and 30 minutes

- 6 (hours) × 60 (minutes) = 360 minutes. So, 360 (minutes) ÷ 4 ($1/4$) = 90 minutes.

Q18. a = £34.64

- Add all of the currency together to reach the answer of £34.64.

Q19. d = 2,440 metres

- Multiply 4 by 610 metres to reach your answer of 2,440 metres.

Q20. c = 120 hours

First of all you need to determine how many 'real' hours he works each day. Subtract the total sum of breaks from 8 hours to reach 6 hours per day. If he works 5 days per week then he is working a total of 30 hours per week. Multiply 30 hours by 4 weeks to reach your answer of 120 hours.

PART 2 OF NUMERICAL REASONING

You have 20 minutes to complete the 15 questions.

Question 1

The following table shows the prices to place different sized advertisements in the main section of a newspaper.

ADVERTISEMENT PRICES		
Size of the Advertisement	Colour	Mono
24 x 10	£12,435	£8,567
22 x 5	£6,437	£4,218
8 x 10	£4,208	£3,987
7 x 5	£2,576	£1,340

How much more does it cost a company to place two 24 × 10 mono advertisements and one 22 × 5 colour advertisement, compared to a company placing three 8 × 10 colour advertisements and one 7 × 5 mono advertisement?

A	B	C	D	E
£5,040	£1,365	£10,460	£9,607	£2,464

Question 2

Below is a table of the total staff at Company A (Staff Distribution).

	HR (%)	Sales (%)	Finance (%)	Media (%)	Distribution (%)	TOTAL (%)
Year 1	21	8	19	32	20	100
Year 2	28	11	17	28	16	100
Year 3	16	21	19	25	18	100
Year 4	13	30	21	11	22	100
Year 5	4	9	25	33	24	100
Year 6	20	27	25	12	16	100

In Year 4, there were 504 people employed in Finance. How many people in total were employed in Year 4 in the department of Sales?

A	B	C	D	E
650	550	840	720	880

Question 3
Below is a pie-chart representing crime in the town of Upton. Based on an estimated 200 crimes, use the pie-chart below to estimate the number of burglary-related crimes.

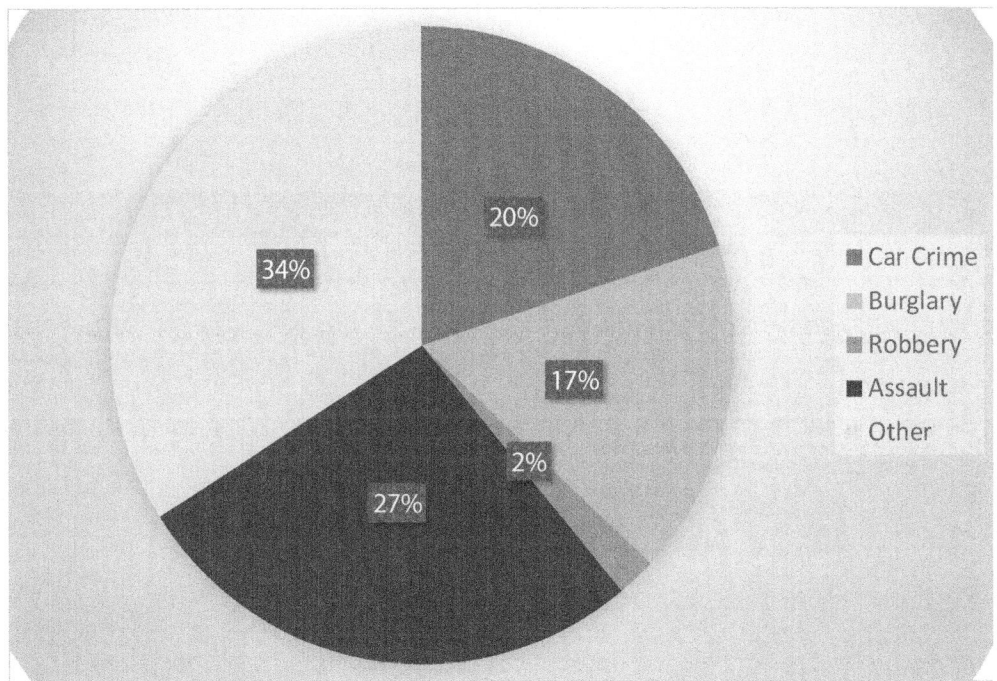

A	B	C	D	E
34	17	27	38	170

Question 4

If I were leaving from Hammersmith, what train time is best to catch if I wish to arrive in Franks Park just before 9 o'clock?

	Train 1	Train 2	Train 3	Train 4
Petersberg	6.45	7.04	------	8.04
Hammersmith	7.00	------	7.45	8.19
St Leonard's Station	7.12	7.20	8.00	------
Mariweather	7.36	7.42	------	8.30
Goldsberg	7.52	------	8.19	8.48
Upperside	8.12	8.04	8.27	9.04
Franks Park	8.30	8.27	8.48	9.28

A	B	C	D	E
7.04	8.04	7.45	7.00	8.19

Question 5

Below is a table listing the percentage changes from 2014 to 2016 for five different companies.

COMPANY	Percentage Change from 2014-2015	Percentage Change from 2015-2016
Company A	+17%	-5%
Company B	+12%	+5%
Company C	-11%	+8%
Company D	-5%	-7%
Company E	+8%	-3%

Using the above table, if company B earned £412,500 in 2014, how much money did the company make in 2016?

A	B	C	D	E
£316,975	£462,000	£415,290	£485,100	£420,000

CHAPTER 4 – NUMERICAL REASONING TESTS

Question 6

In a survey, people had to choose either A, B, C or D.

The percentages for A, C and D are shown below.

A	B	C	D
25%		30%	15%

320 people chose A. How many people chose option B?

A	B	C	D	E
215	384	429	502	301

Question 7

The graph shows respondents' answers when asked what their most frequent form of technological communication was.

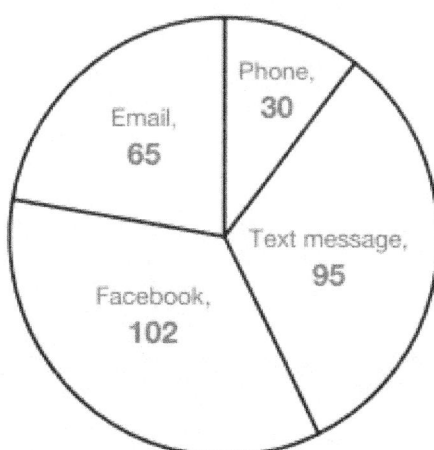

Among the respondents, 75% of all respondents said that it was easier to get in touch with someone through technological communications based on convenience.

How many people said that it was easier to use technological communications based on convenience?

A	B	C	D	E
212	119	227	219	176

Question 8

The following sign shows the opening times for a zoo.

How many months of the year does the zoo close during weekdays?

A	B	C	D	E
4	5	6	3	2

Question 9

Using the table to question 8, answer the following question. Kelly goes to the zoo in July. She arrives at 2pm. How many hours can she spend there until it closes?

A	B	C	D	E
3 hours	1 hour	6 hours	5 hours	4 hours

Question 10

Using the table to question 8, answer the following question. Marcus has a season ticket for 2017, allowing him multiple visits at a reduced price. He visits the zoo the following times throughout the year:

- Once in January, arriving when the park opens and leaving 2 hours before last admission.

- Once in May, arriving at 3:00pm and leaving an hour before closing time.
- Once in July, arriving one hour after the park opens and leaving 5 hours before closing time.
- Once in August, arriving at 4pm and staying until closing time.

How much time did Marcus spend in the zoo in 2017 in hours and minutes?

A	B	C	D	E
12 hours	12 hours and 30 minutes	10 hours	11 hours and 30 minutes	14 hours

Question 11

Abe has some spare pieces of wood in his shed. He is trying to work out if he can make a box with them. Below is a chart showing some of their sizes. Complete the table.

Area (cm²)	Perimeter (cm)	Length (cm)	Width (cm)
36		12	
		6	5
64			8

Question 12

See below a table of values representing the formula 9 (x + 5). Some of the boxes have already been filled in. Using the values already in the table, fill in the missing gaps.

x	9 (x + 5)
10	135
	81
6	

Question 13

The bar chart below shows the number of people who applied for a Sales Assistant job. The job was advertised for one week, and the bars on the chart represent each day of the week up until the closing date.

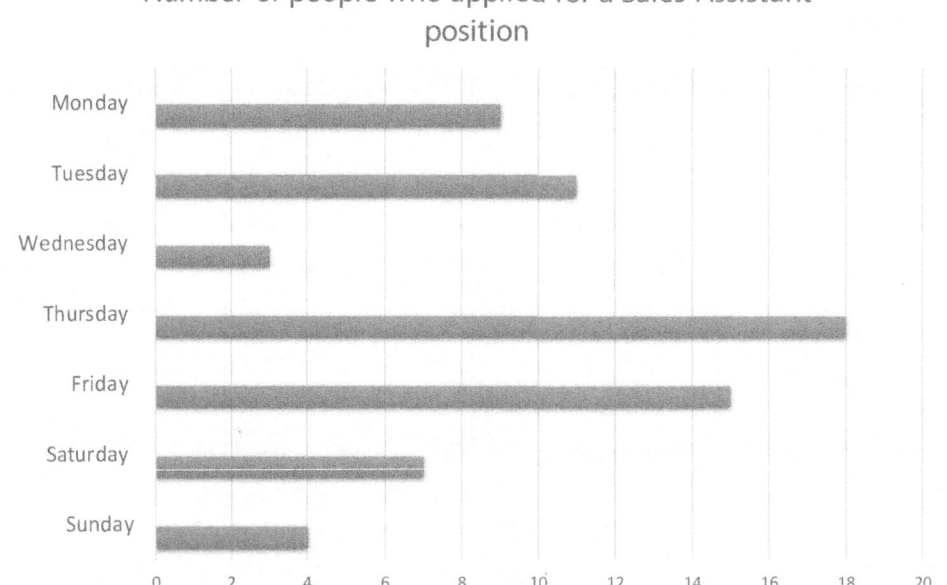

On Wednesday, 3 people applied for the job.

Work out how many people applied for the Sales Assistant position overall.

A	B	C	D	E
58	59	63	67	72

Question 14

A psychologist works on a fixed charge depending on the duration of each session.

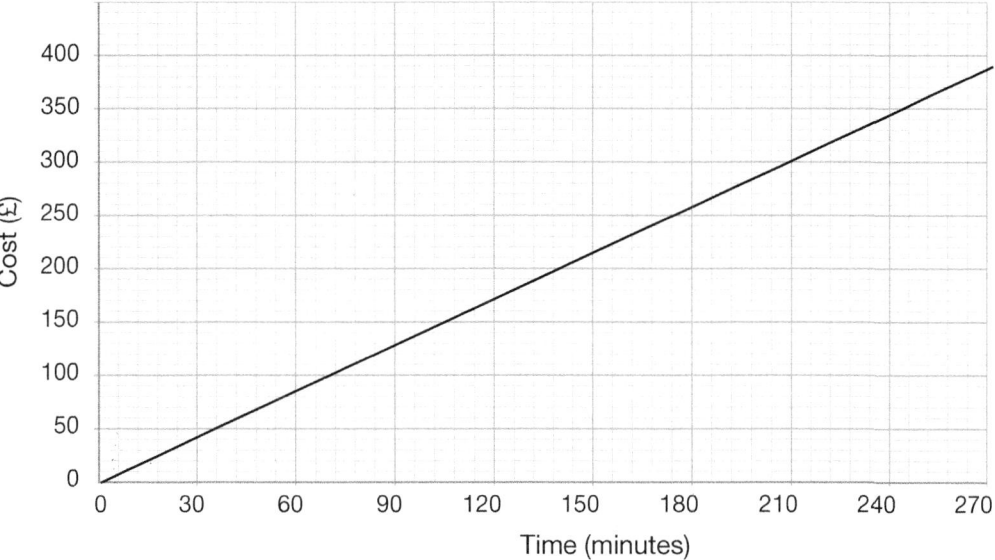

How much does the psychologist charge for 15 minutes?

A	B	C	D	E
£10	£15	£25	£50	£30

Question 15

Using the graph from question 14, answer the following question. If a client comes for a 90 minute session twice a week, for five weeks, how much will he have to pay?

A	B	C	D	E
£1,100	£1,250	£1,400	£1,300	£1,500

ANSWERS TO NUMERICAL REASONING TEST (PART 2)

Q1. D = £9,607

- Step 1 = first company places orders for two 24 × 10 mono advertisements = 2 × £8,567 = £17,134 and one 22 × 5 colour advertisement = 1 × £6,437 = 6,437

- Step 2 = 6,437 + 17,134 = £23,571

- Step 3 = second company places orders for three 8 × 10 colour advertisements = 3 × 4,208 = 12,624 and one 7 × 5 mono advertisement = 1 × £1,340 = £1,340

- Step 3 = £12,624 + £1,340 = £13,964

- Step 4 = difference between the first company and the second company = £23,571 – £13.964 = £9,607

Q2. D = 720

In order to work out the number of people working in Sales in Year 4, you need to work out the total number of employees in that year.

- So, 504 (number of people employed in Finance) × 100 ÷ 21 (percentage of Finance) = 2400.

- So, 2400 ÷ 100 × 30 (number of employees in Sales) = 720.

Q3. A = 34

- 200 ÷ 100 × 17 = 34

CHAPTER 4 – NUMERICAL REASONING TESTS

Q4. C = 7.45

If you were leaving from Hammersmith, that means you need to focus on the second row of train times (don't count the train times from Petersberg). You want to arrive in Franks Park just before 9 o'clock, so you would need to catch the 7.45 train from Hammersmith.

Q5. D = £485,100

According to the table, if the amount of sales at Company B was £412,500 for 2014, then it was 12 percent greater for 2015, which is 112 percent of that amount. So, 412,500 ÷ 100 × 112 = 462,000. From 2015 to 2016, the company saw a 5% increase, which is 105% of the previous month. So, 462,000 ÷ 100 × 105 = 485,100. So, the correct answer is £485,100.

Q6. B = 384

- First you need to work out how many people took the survey in total: 320 (people who chose A) × 100 ÷ 25(%) = 1280.
- Next, you need to work out the missing percentage for B. 100(%) – 25(%) – 30(%) – 15(%) = 30(%).
- So, B is going to be 30% of the total: 1280 ÷ 100 × 30 = 384.

Q7. D = 219

- First, you need to add up all the respondents who took part in the survey: 65 + 30 + 95 + 102 = 292.
- Next, you need to work out 75% of 292: 292 ÷ 100 × 75 = 219.
- So, 219 respondents said they use certain technological communications for convenience.

Q8. C = 6 months

- September, October, November, December, January and February.

Q9. C = 6 hours

- 2pm until 8pm.

Q10. B = 12 hours and 30 minutes

- 10am to 12 noon = 2 hours
- 3pm to 4:30pm = 1 hour 30 minutes
- 10am to 3pm = 5 hours
- 4pm to 8pm = 4 hours
- 2 + 1.5 + 5 + 4 = 12.5 (12 hours and 30 minutes).

Q11.

Area (cm^2)	Perimeter (cm)	Length (cm)	Width (cm)
36	30	12	3
30	22	6	5
64	32	8	8

Q12.

x	9 (x + 5)
10	135
4	81
6	99

- (4 + 5 × 9 = 81)
- (6 + 5 × 9 = 99)

Q13. D = 67

Each line on the graph represents '2'.

- Monday = 9
- Tuesday = 11
- Wednesday = 3
- Thursday = 18
- Friday = 15
- Saturday 7
- Sunday = 4
- 9 + 11 + 3 + 18 + 15 + 7 + 4 = 67

Q14. C = £25

Using the graph, you need to find the '15' minutes along the bottom of the graph (because the graph goes up in 30 minutes, you need to find half of 30). Once you've found the 15 minutes, work your way up until you reach the black line: this will tell you how much it costs for 15 minutes.

Q15. D = £1,300

- £130 × 2 (number of times per week) = £260
- £260 × 5 (five weeks) = £1,300

Now that you've completed sample questions for numerical reasoning, let's take a look at the next section – spatial reasoning.

CHAPTER 5 — SPATIAL REASONING TESTS

RAF DEFENCE APTITUDE ASSESSMENT

During the RAF Defence Aptitude Assessment, you will be required to undertake a Spatial Reasoning Test.

The definition of spatial reasoning is as follows:

> "The ability to interpret and make drawings from mental images and visualise movement or change in those images."

During the DAA, you will be confronted with a number of spatial reasoning questions, and the only effective way to prepare for them is to try as many sample questions as you can.

In the real test, you will be given 4 minutes to answer 10 questions for part 1. For part 2, you will be given 3 minutes to answer 10 questions.

SPATIAL REASONING PRACTICE QUESTION 1

Take a look at the following three shapes. Note the letters on the side of each shape.

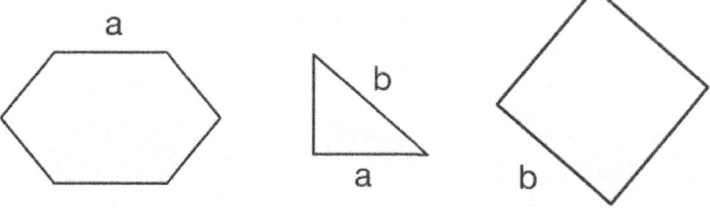

Your task is to join all three shapes together using the corresponding letters. This would make the following shape:

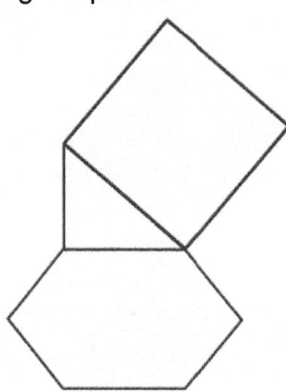

CHAPTER 5 – SPATIAL REASONING TESTS

PART 1 OF SPATIAL REASONING

You have 4 minutes to complete the 10 questions.

Question 1

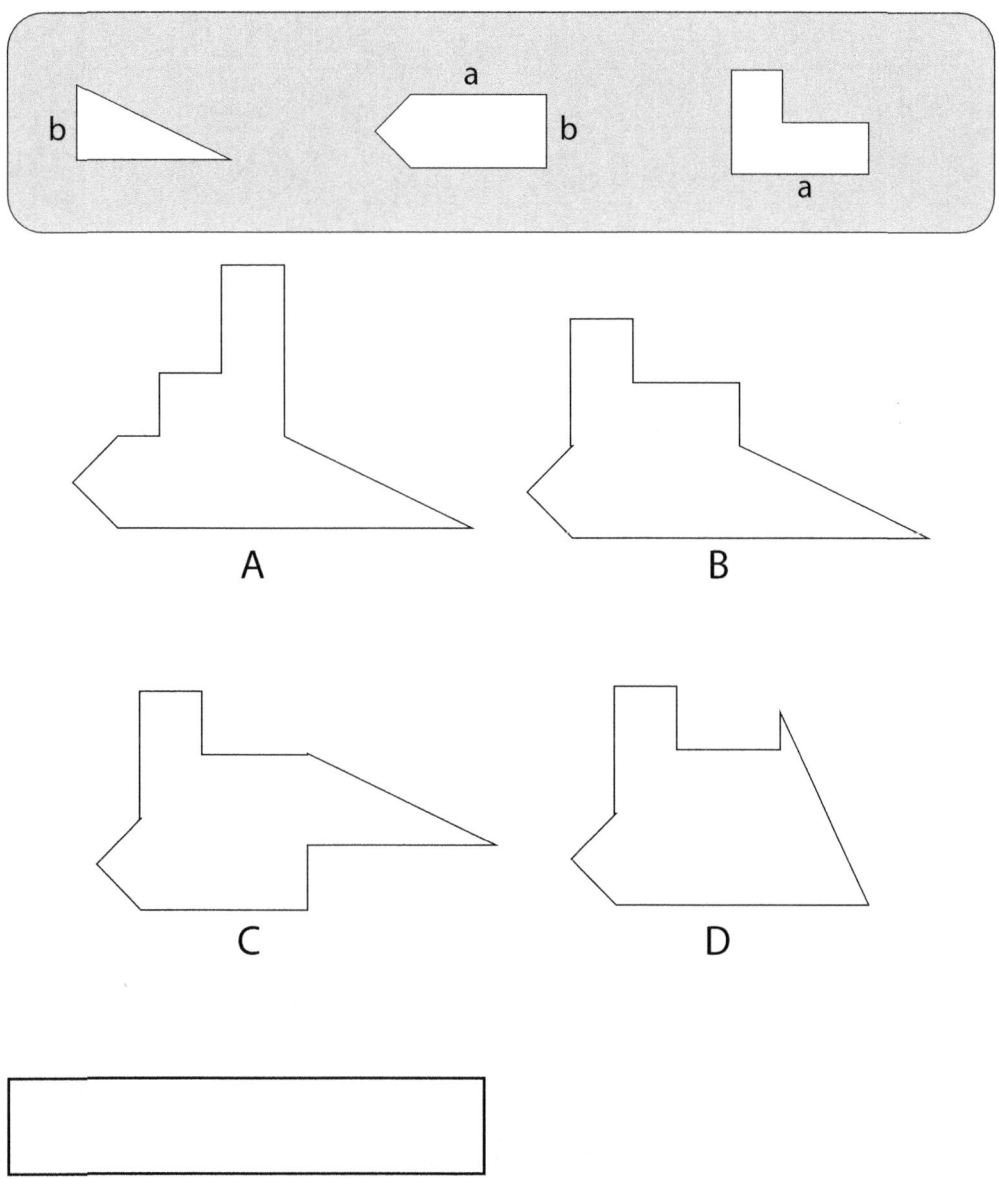

RAF DEFENCE APTITUDE ASSESSMENT

Question 2

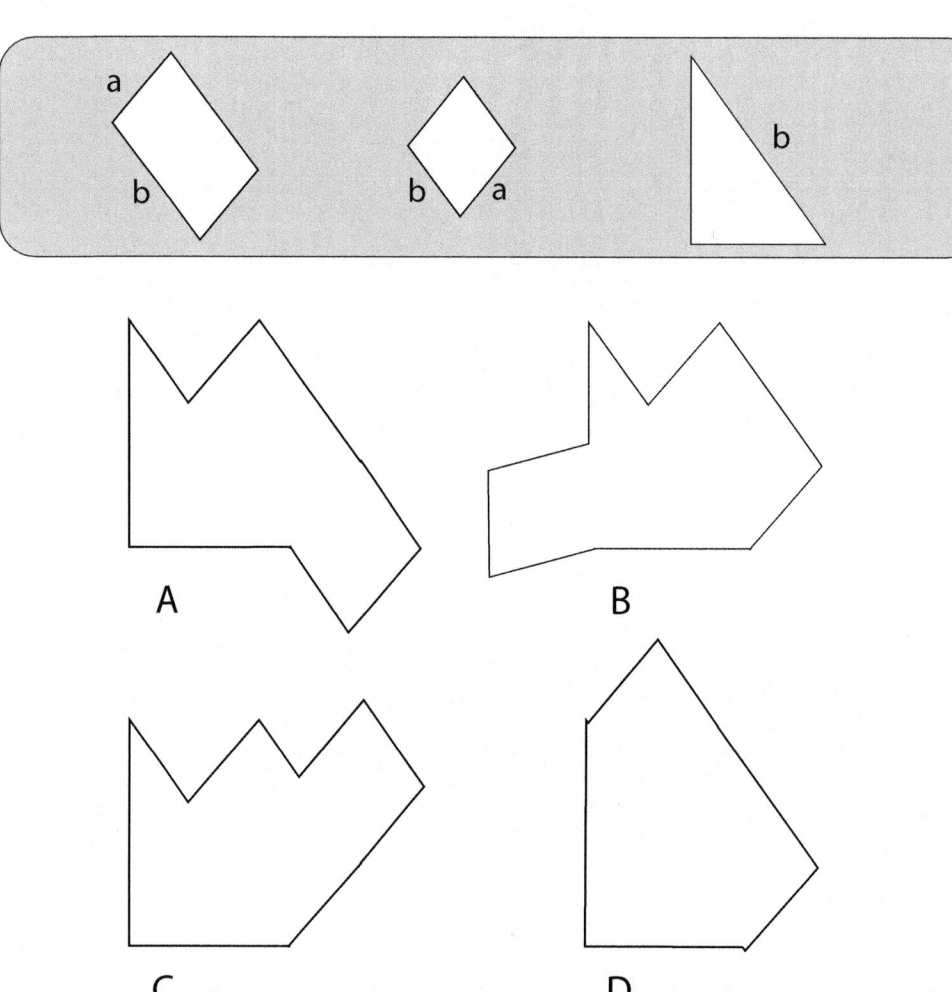

Question 3

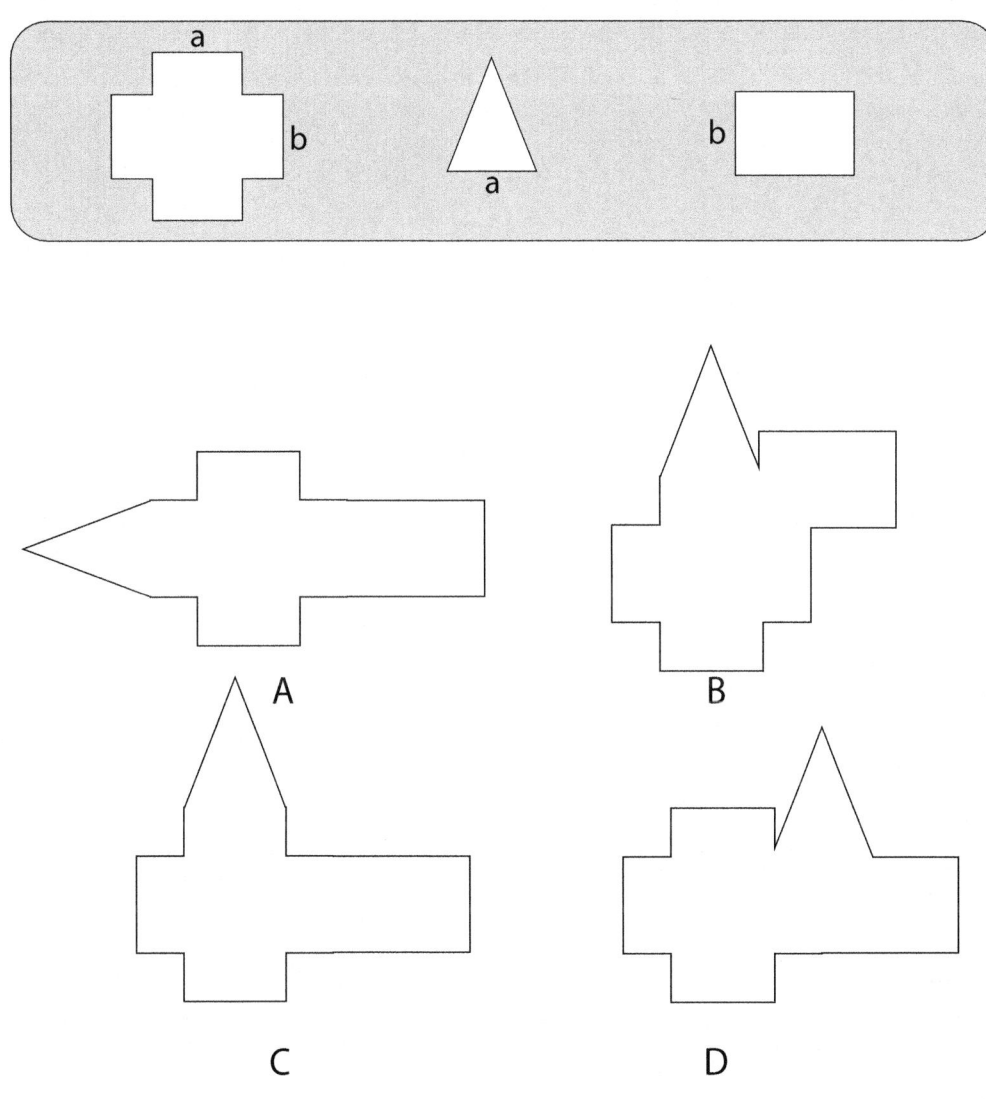

Question 4

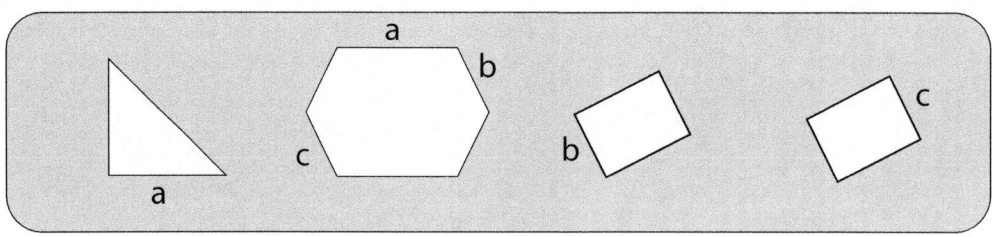

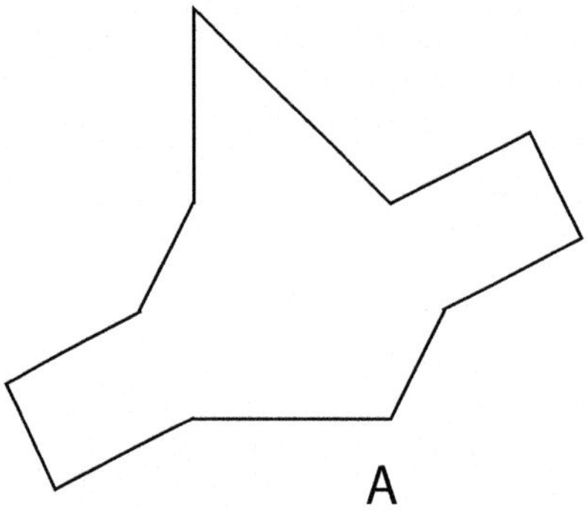

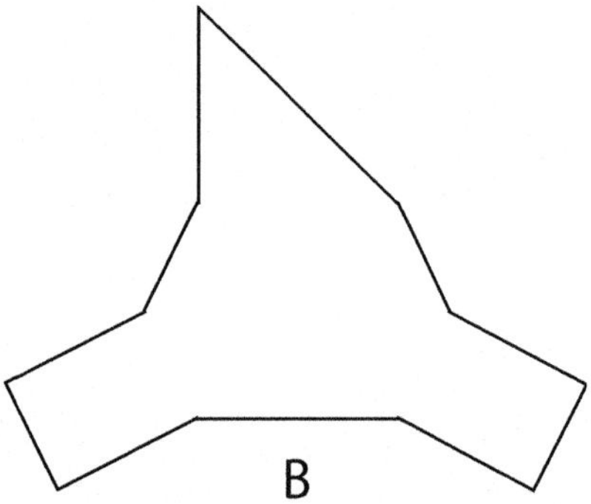

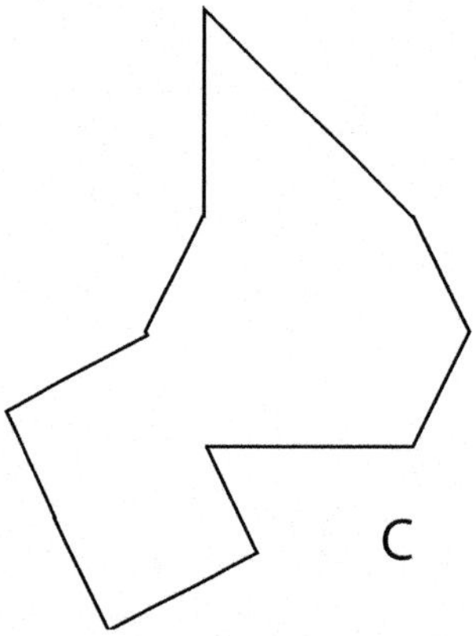

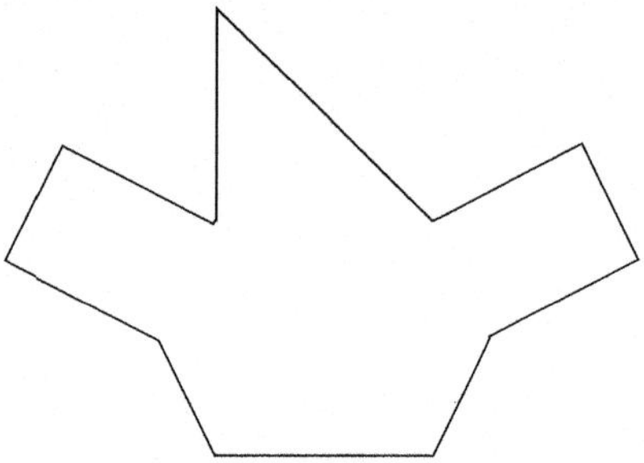

Question 5

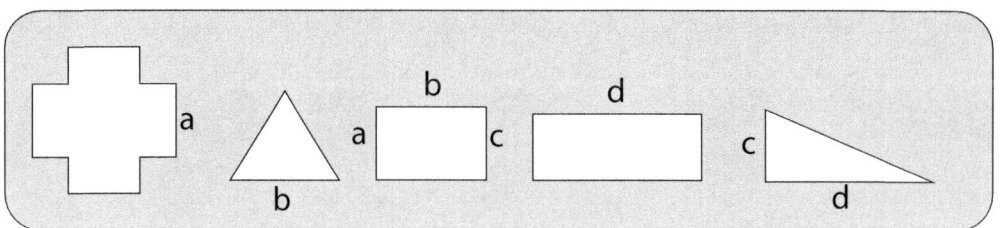

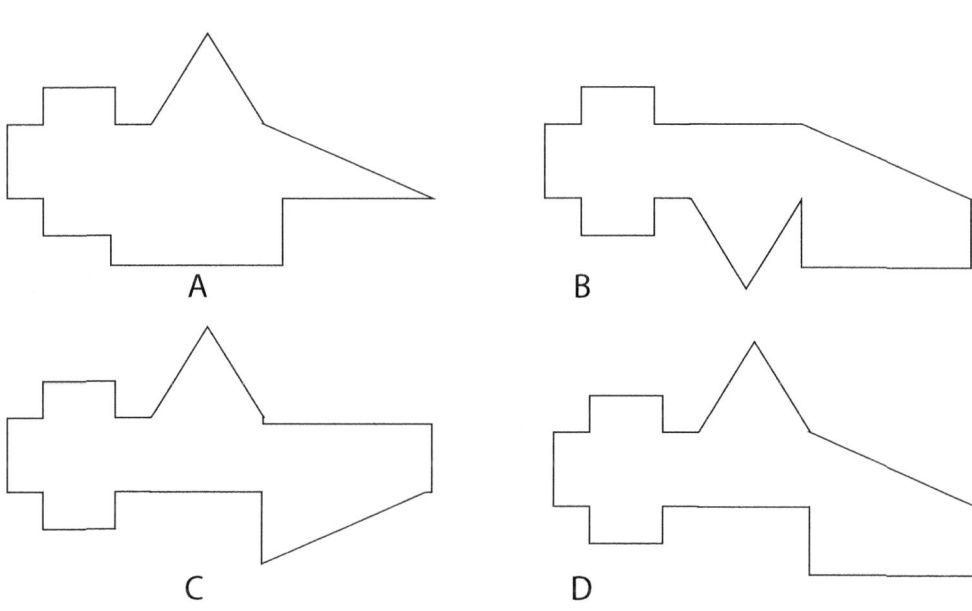

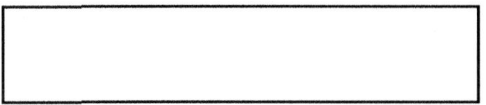

Question 6

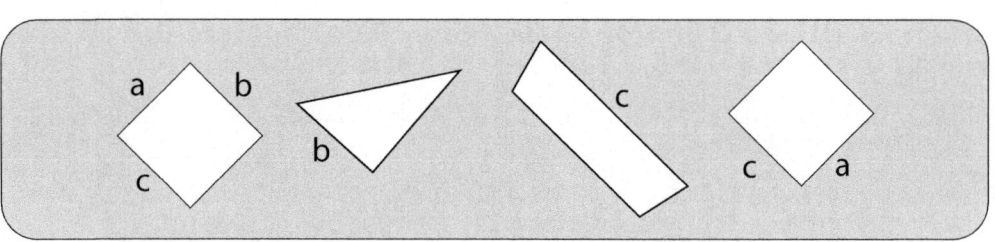

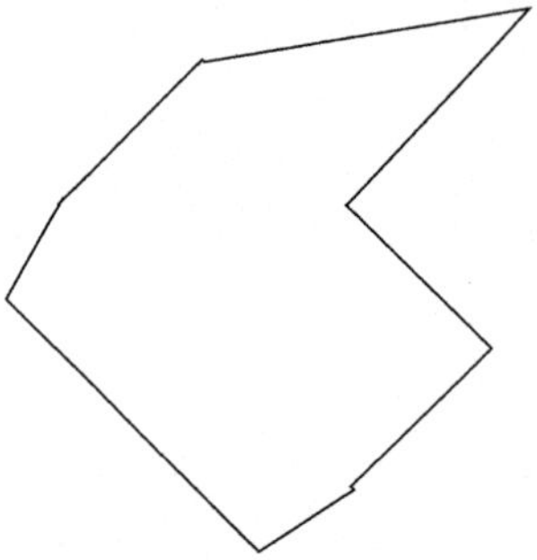

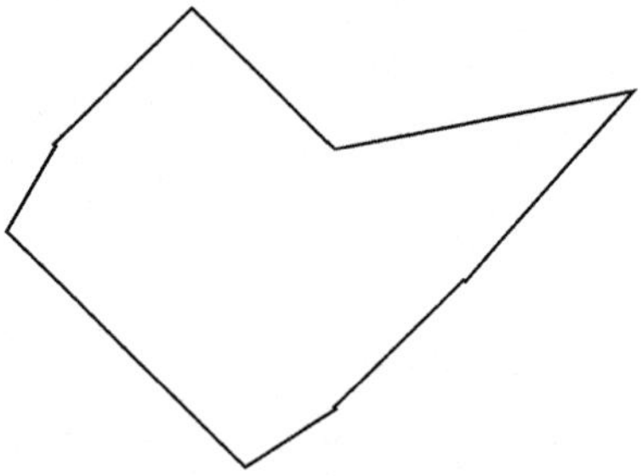

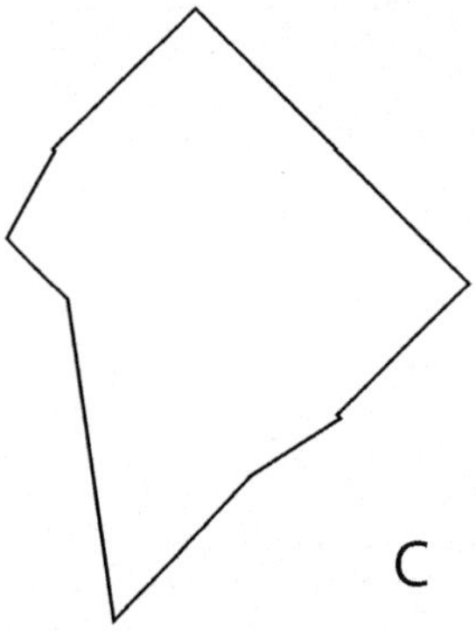

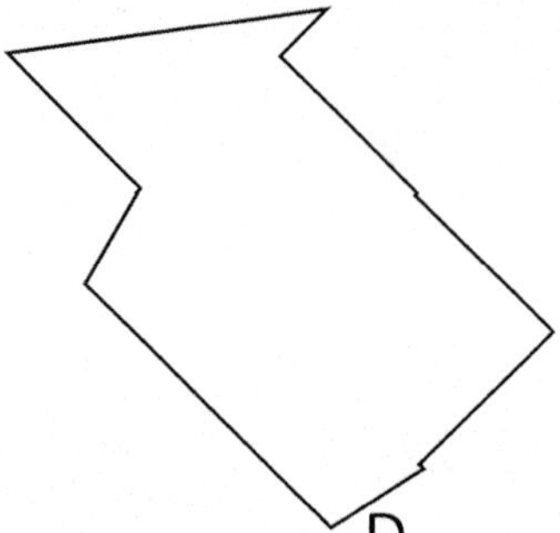

Question 7

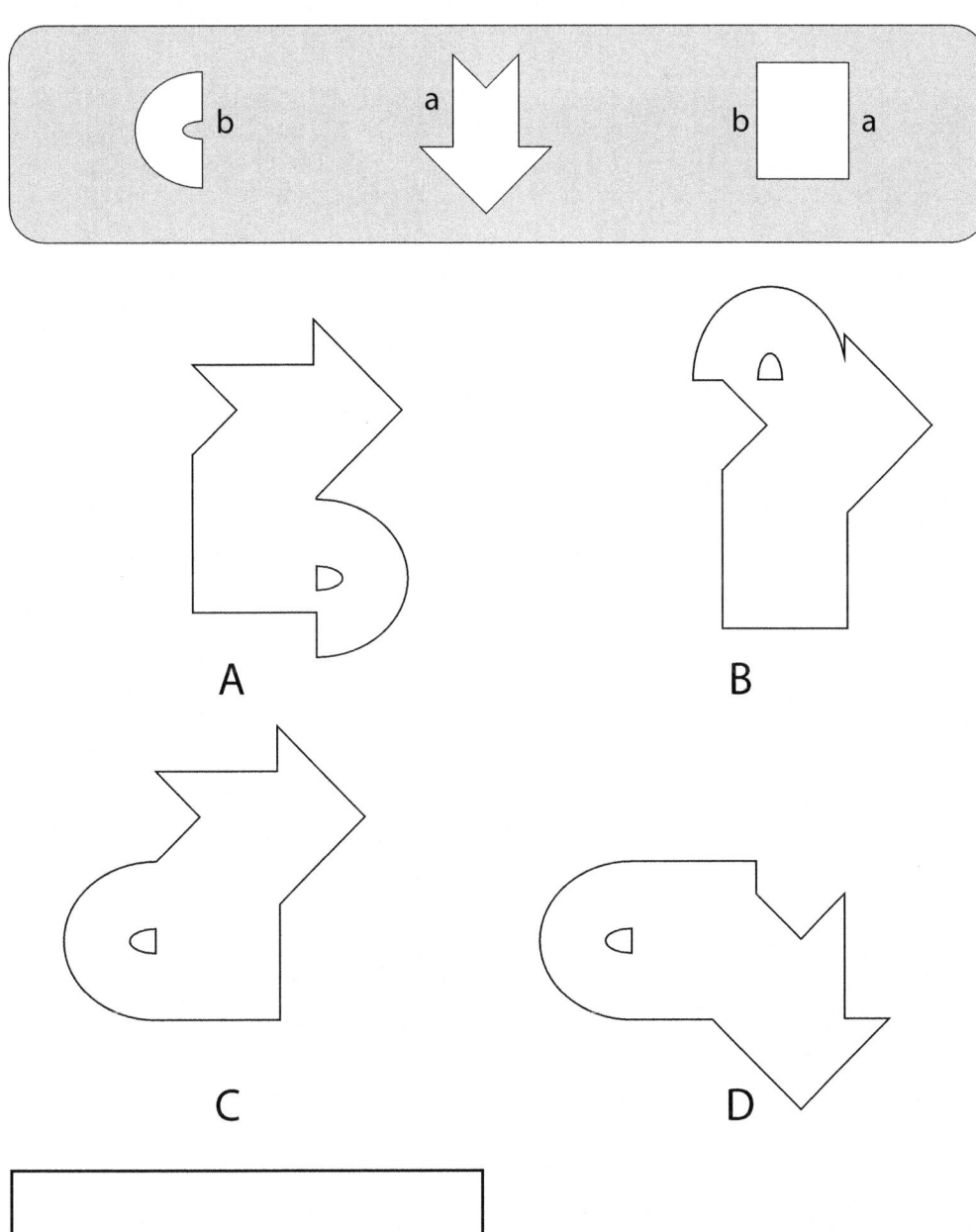

Question 8

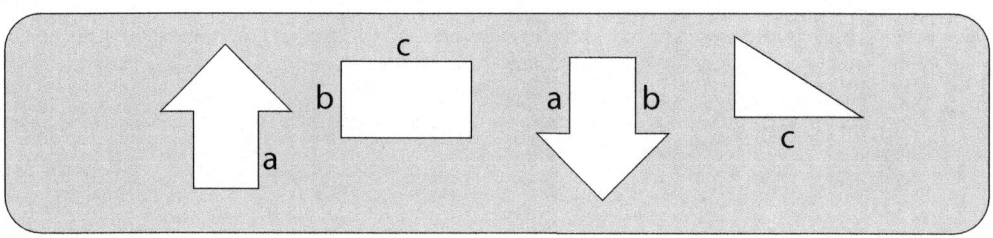

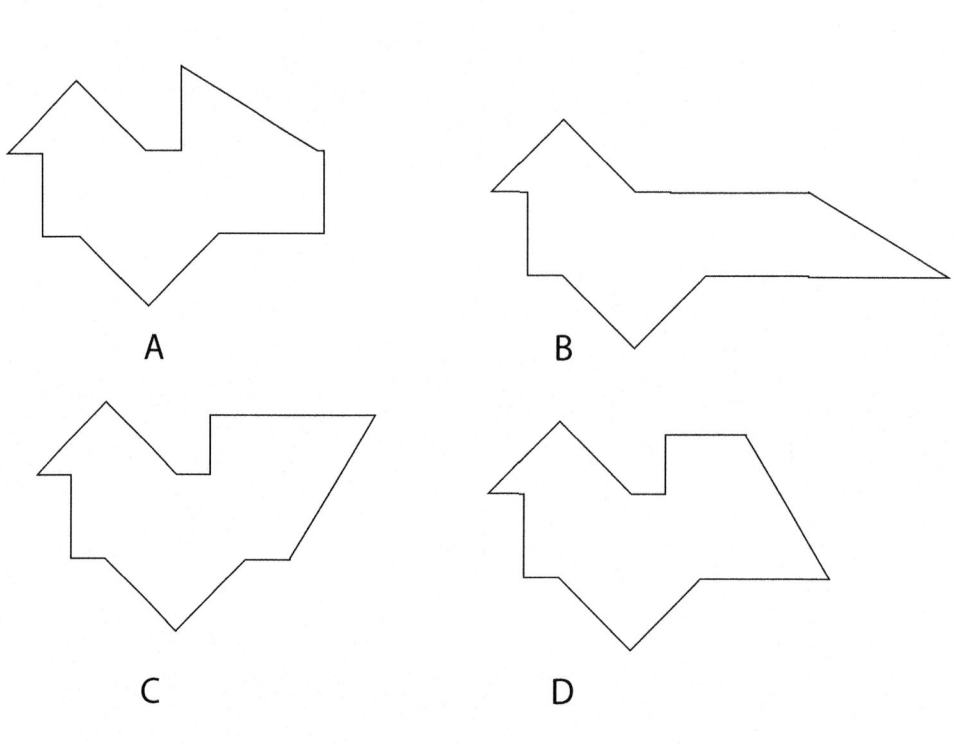

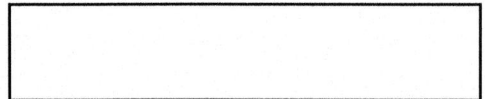

Question 9

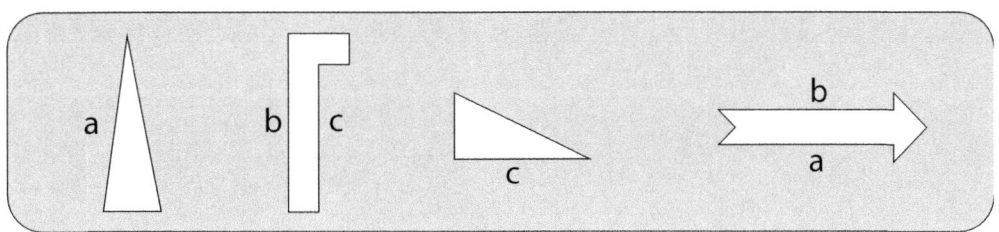

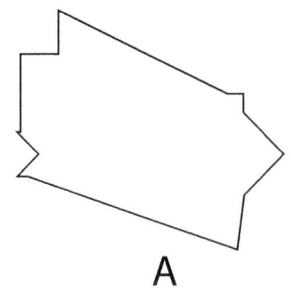

A

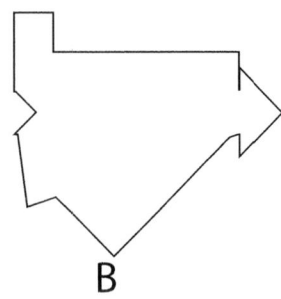

B

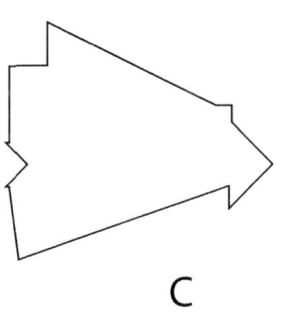

C

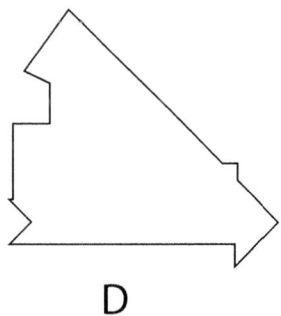

D

Question 10

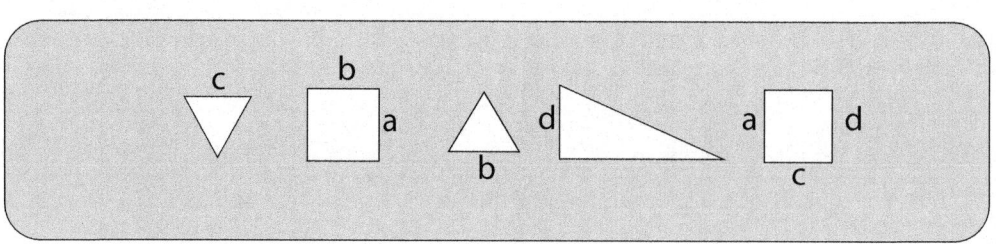

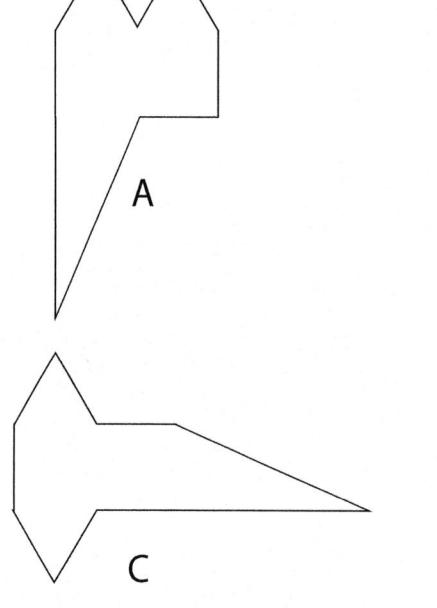

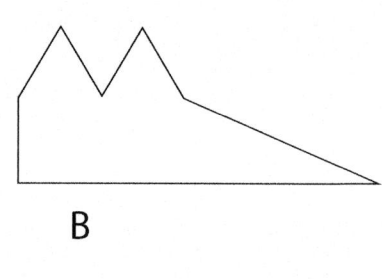

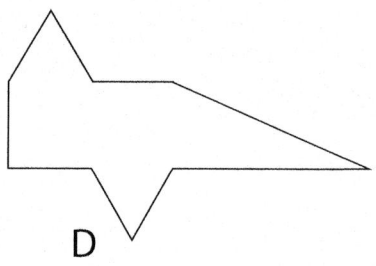

CHAPTER 5 – SPATIAL REASONING TESTS

ANSWERS TO SPATIAL REASONING TEST (PART 1)

Q1. B

Q2. D

Q3. C

Q4. A

Q5. D

Q6. B

Q7. D

Q8. A

Q9. C

Q10. D

SPATIAL REASONING PRACTICE QUESTION 2

Look at the two objects below.

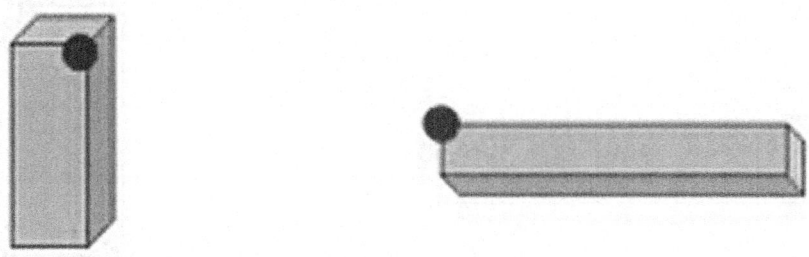

You now have to decide which of the four answer options provided demonstrates both objects rotated with the dot remaining in the SAME corner as found on the original objects.

Look at the answer options below.

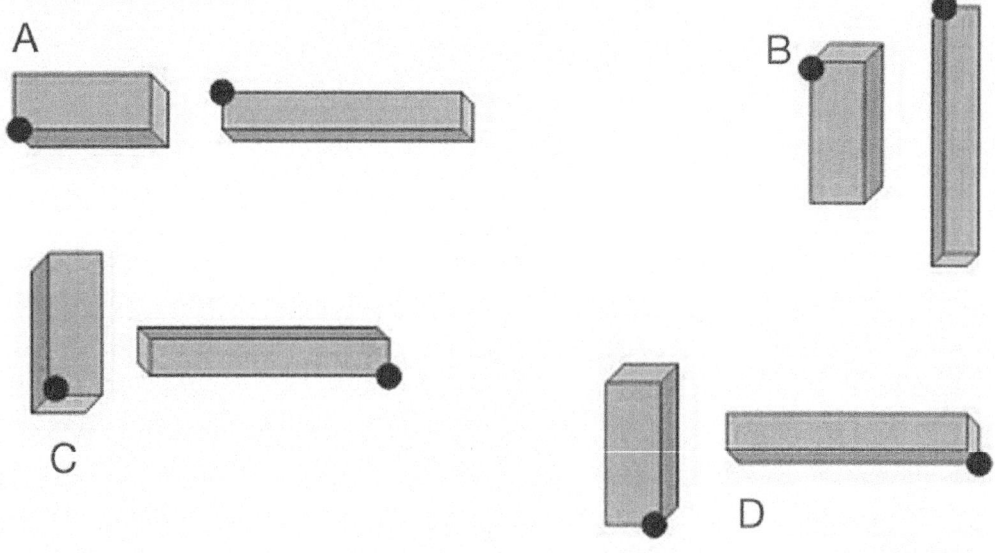

The correct answer is **C**. This is because BOTH objects have been rotated 180°.

Remember, the objects have to rotate EXACTLY the same amount!

CHAPTER 5 – SPATIAL REASONING TESTS

PART 2 OF SPATIAL REASONING

You have 3 minutes to complete the 10 questions.

Question 1

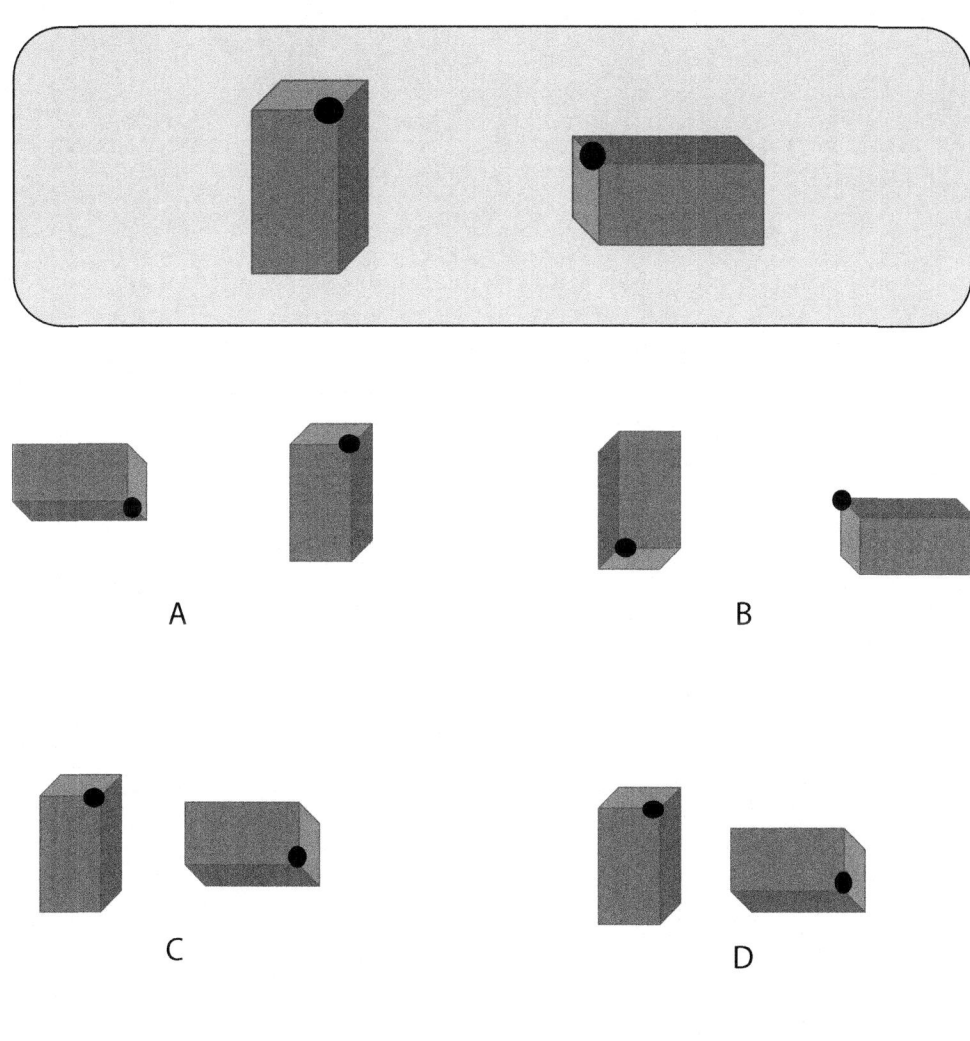

Question 2

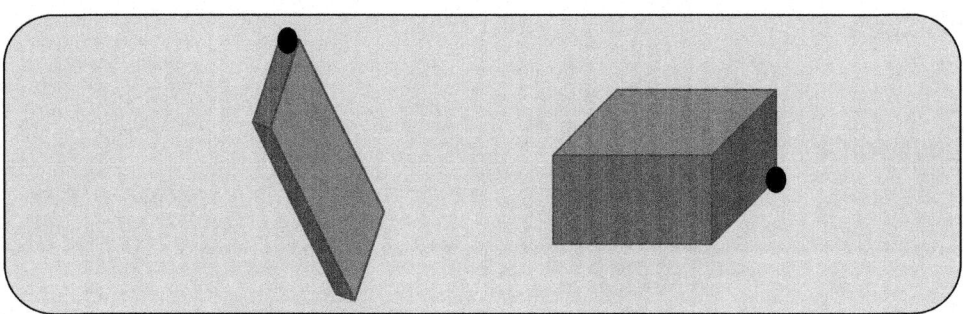

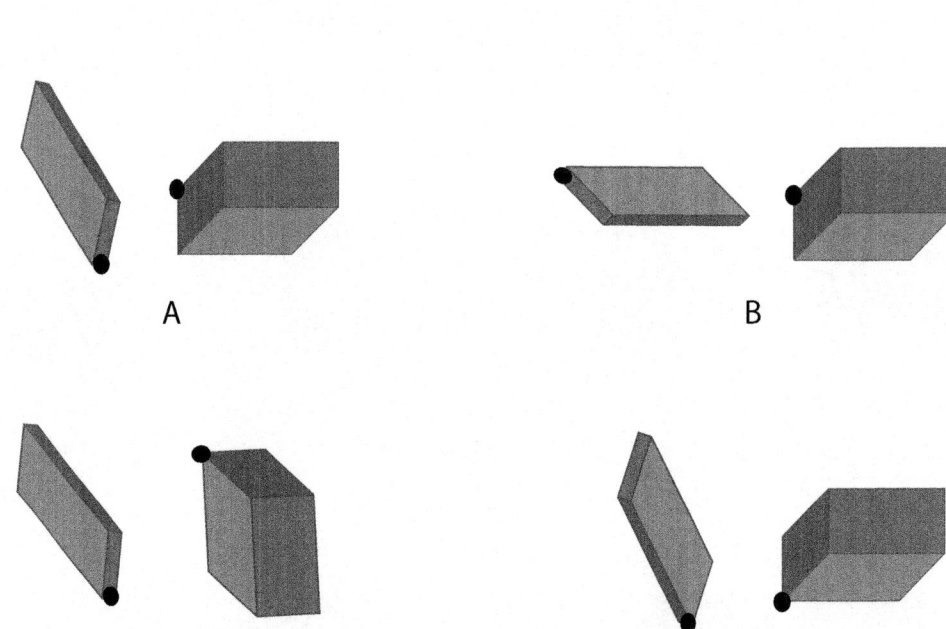

Question 3

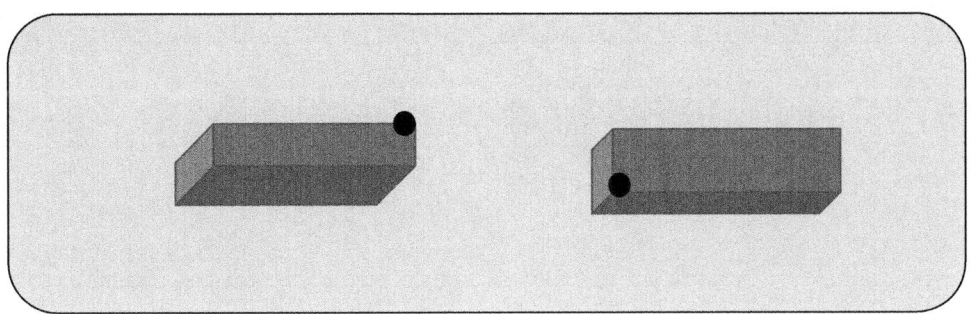

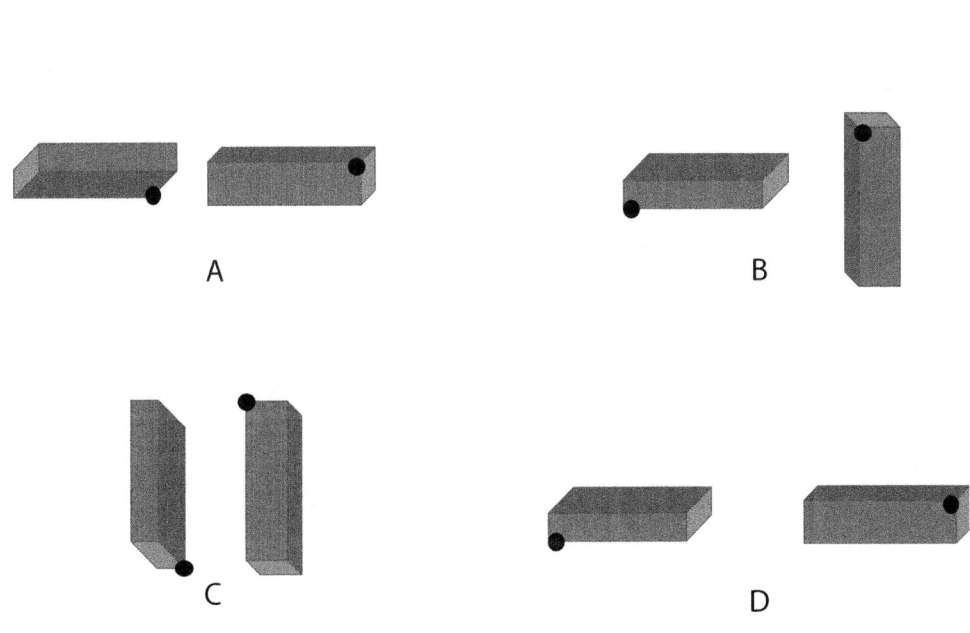

Question 4

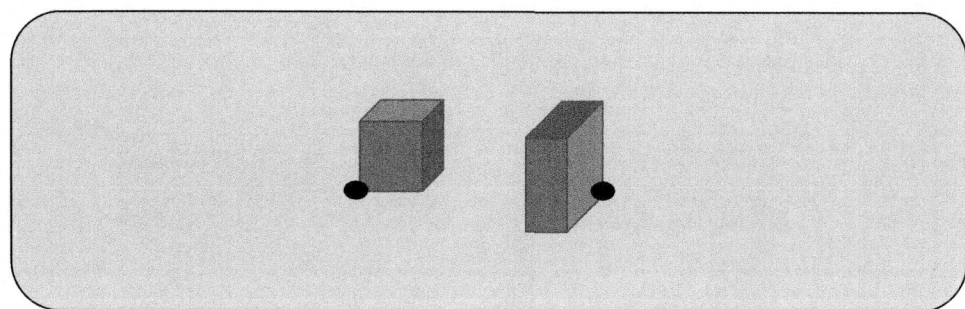

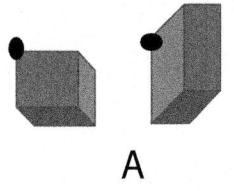

A

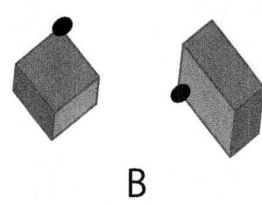

B

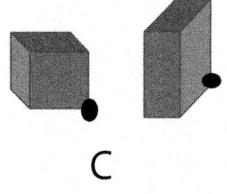

C

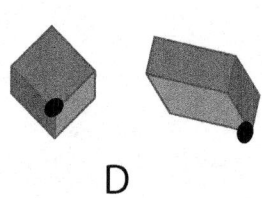

D

Question 5

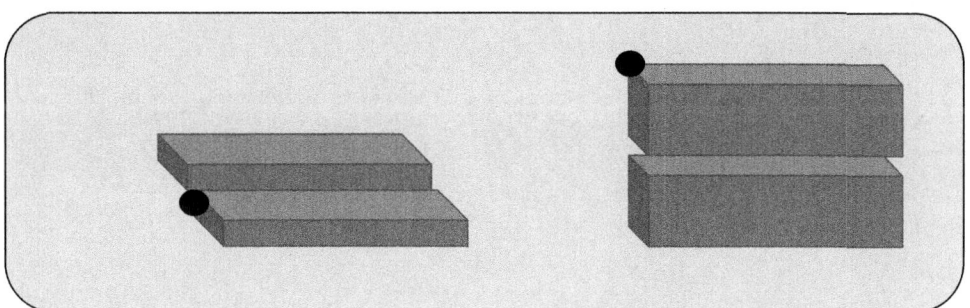

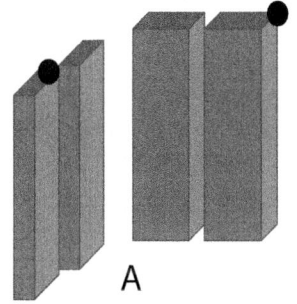

A

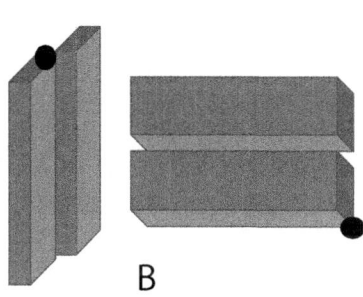

B

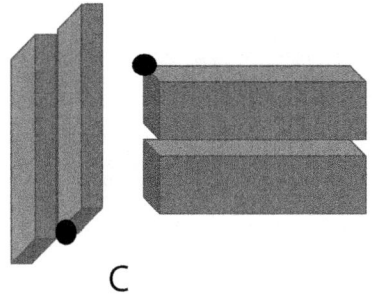

C

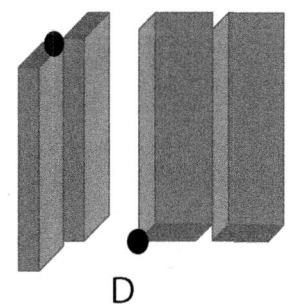

D

Question 6

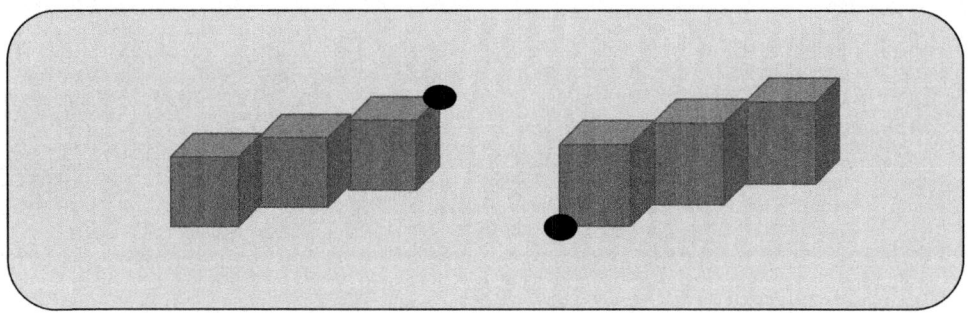

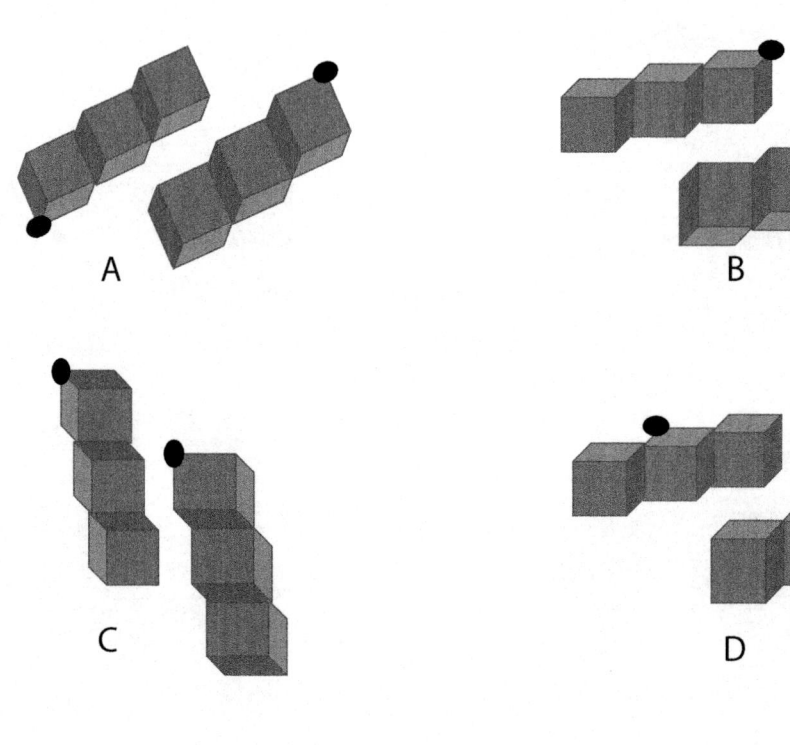

Question 7

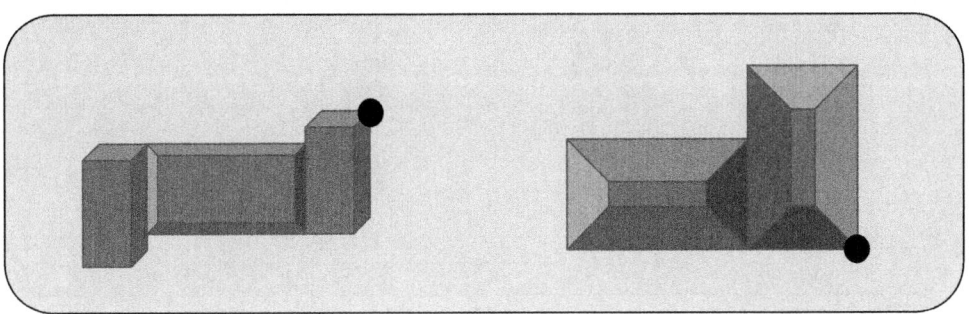

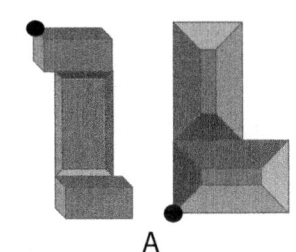
A

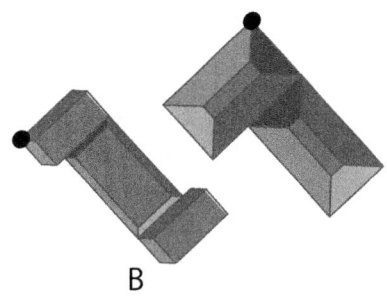
B

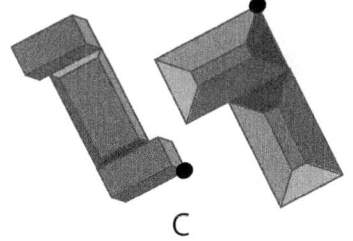
C

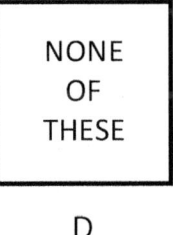

NONE
OF
THESE

D

Question 8

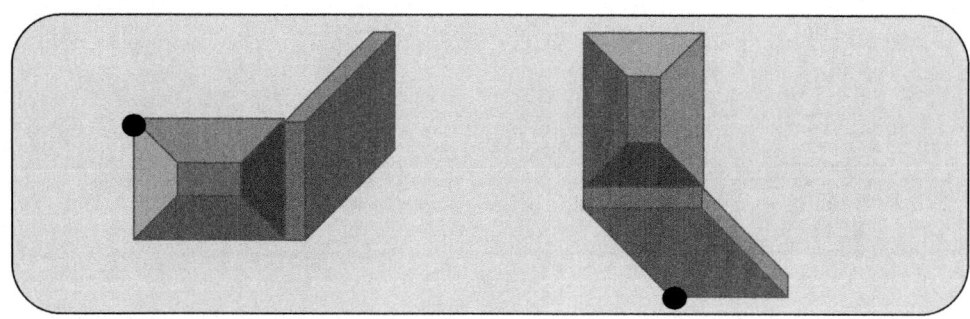

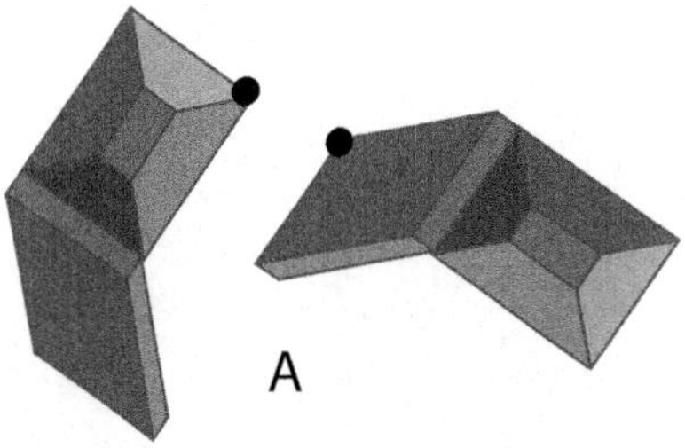

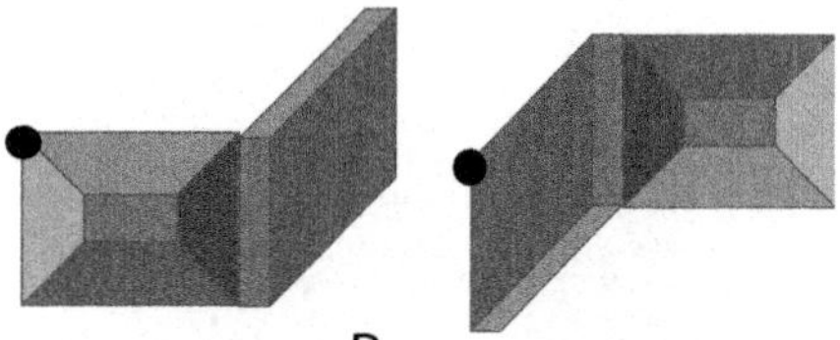

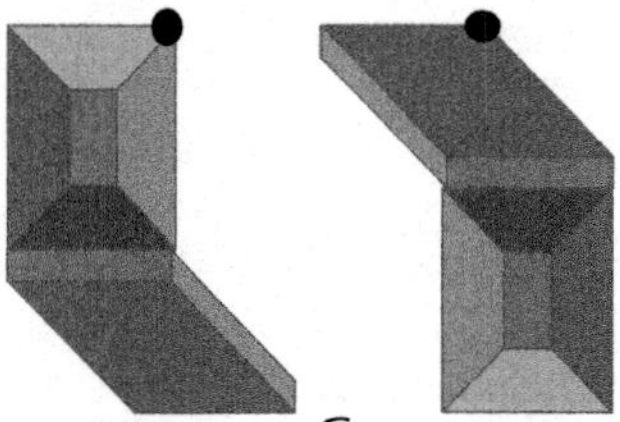

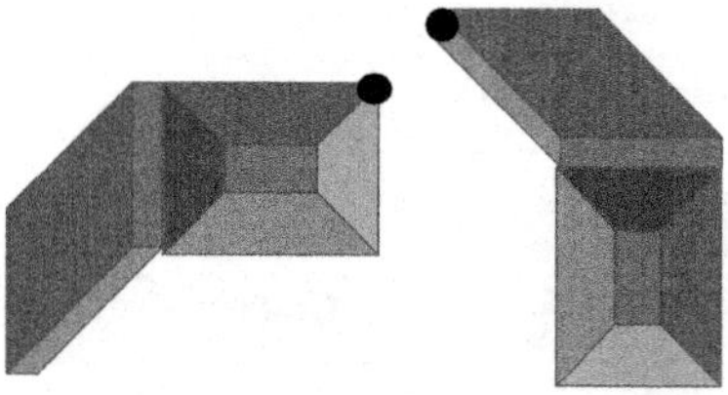

Question 9

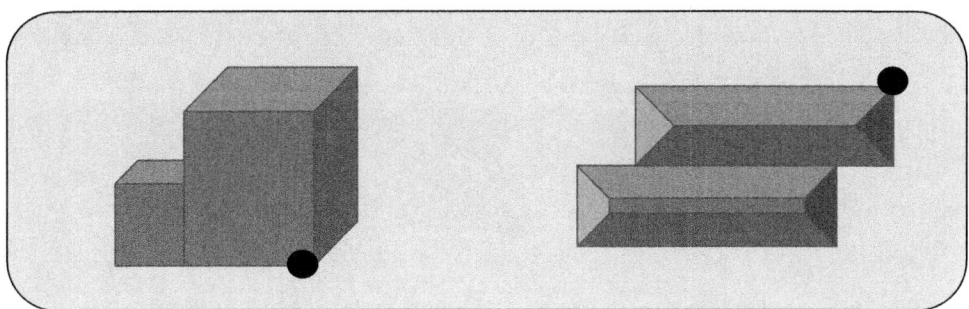

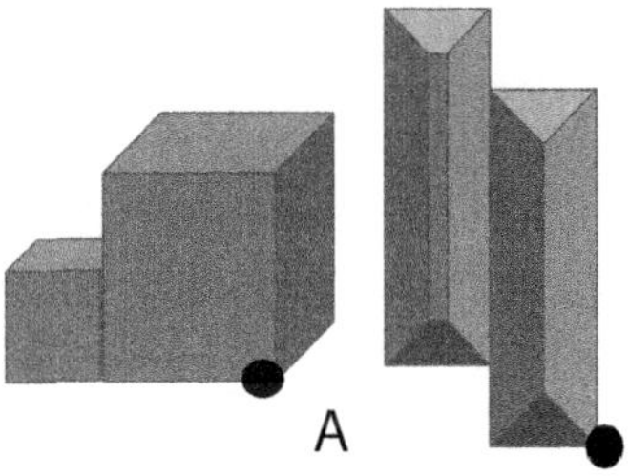

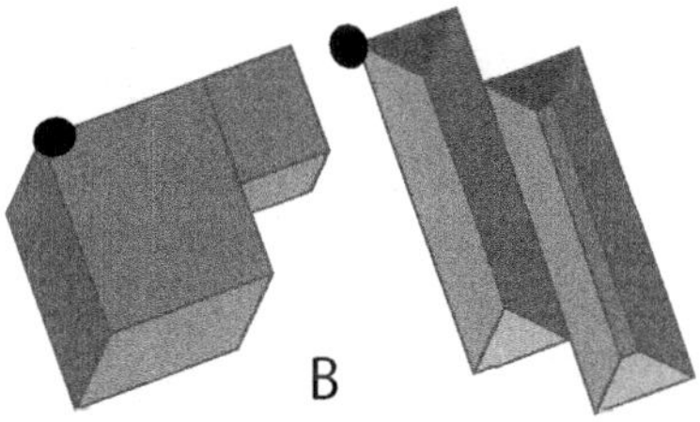

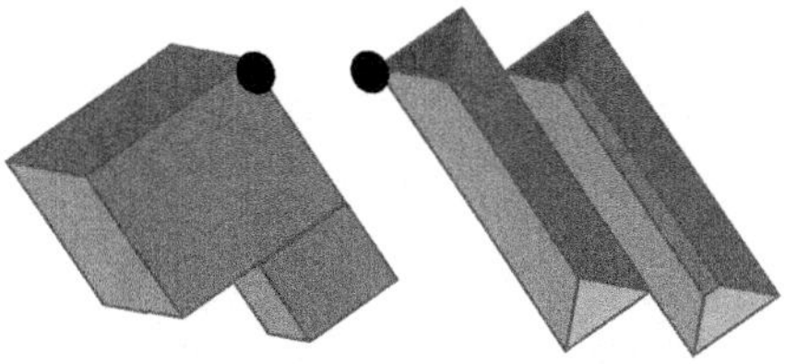

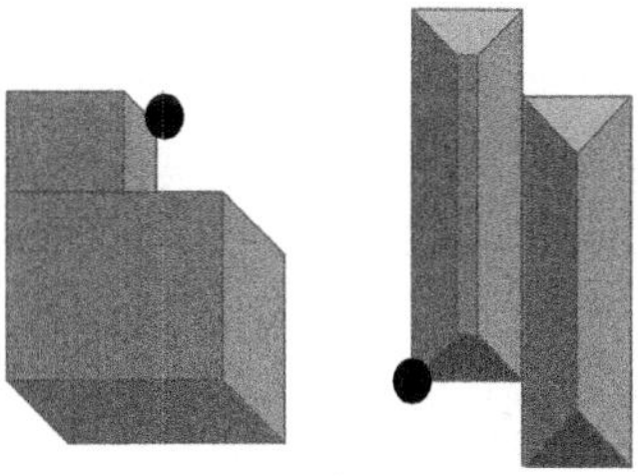

Question 10

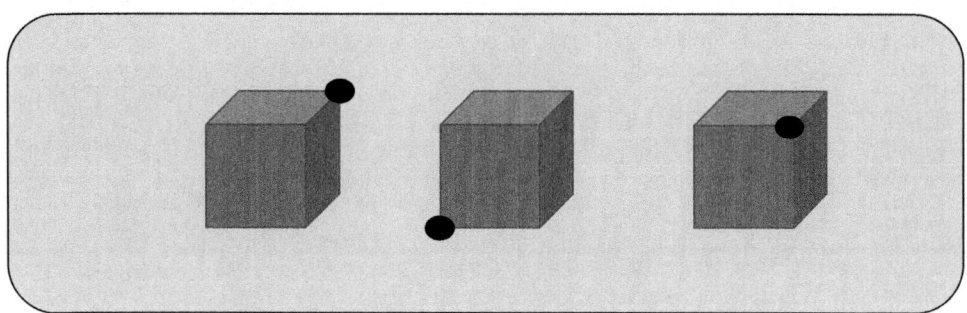

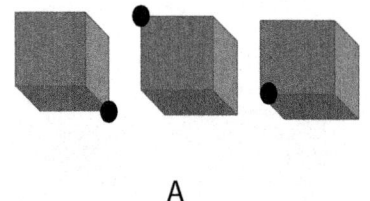

A

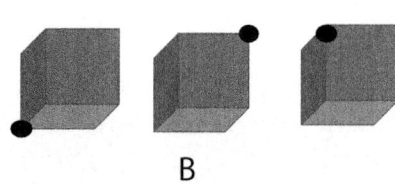

B

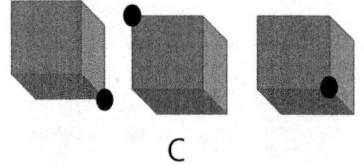

C

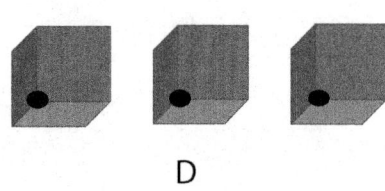

D

CHAPTER 5 – SPATIAL REASONING TESTS

ANSWERS TO SPATIAL REASONING TEST (PART 2)

Q1. A

Q2. A

Q3. D

Q4. B

Q5. A

Q6. A

Q7. B

Q8. A

Q9. C

Q10. C

Now that you've completed sample questions for spatial reasoning, let's take a look at the next section – work rate assessments.

CHAPTER 6 — WORK RATE TESTS

100 RAF DEFENCE APTITUDE ASSESSMENT

During the DAA, you will be required to undertake a Work Rate Test. This form of test assesses your ability to work quickly and accurately whilst carrying out routine tasks; something which is integral to the role of an Airman/Airwoman.

WORK RATE PRACTICE QUESTION

Before we move on to the test questions, let's take a look at a sample question.

To begin with, study the following grid. In the grid, you will be able to see different numbers, letters and symbols.

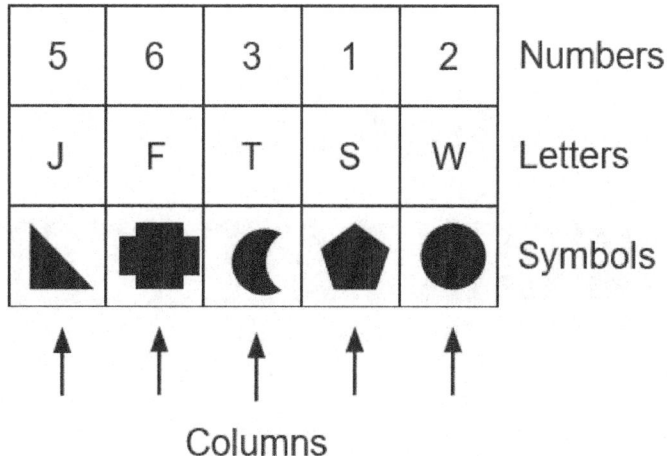

For these questions, you will be given a code consisting of numbers, letters and/or symbols. Your task is to look at the answer options and decide which code has been taken from the **SAME** columns as the original code.

For example, take a look at the following code: **563**

Now look at the five alternatives.

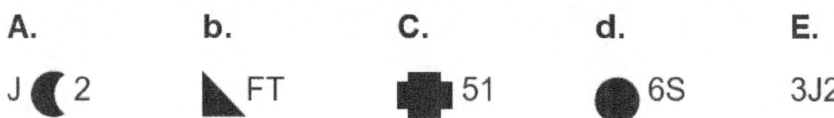

The question is: which code (A-E) has been taken from the **SAME** columns as the code 563?

You can see that the answer is in fact B. The reason for this is that the code has been taken from the **SAME** columns as the original code of 563.

PART 1 OF WORK RATE

You have 10 minutes to complete the 10 questions.

Question 1

Which of the answers below is an alternative to the code **4H9**?

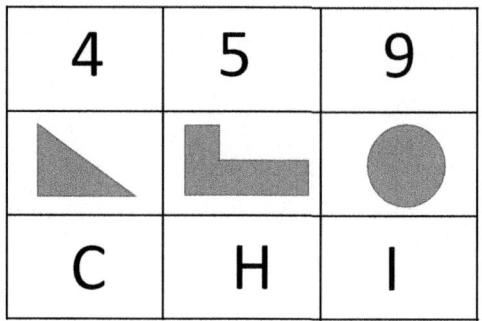

A. C 5 ▙ B. 4 5 H C. ●C I D. C 5 ●

☐

Question 2

Which of the answers below is an alternative to the code **J1X**?

A. ● 9 1 B. 5E9 C. ●▙1 D. 9 1 ●

☐

CHAPTER 6 – WORK RATE TESTS

Question 3

Which of the answers below is an alternative to the code **7B6**?

U	5	✚
✖	●	B
6	7	V

A. 7 U V   B. U 7 B   C. ● V ✖   D. ✖ ● ✚

Question 4

Which of the answers below is an alternative to the code **CB3**?

A	B	C
3	9	✦
▬	■	7

A. A 7 9   B. ▬ B ✦   C. 3 B ■   D. ✦ 9 A

Question 5

Which of the answers below is an alternative to the code **6EYX**?

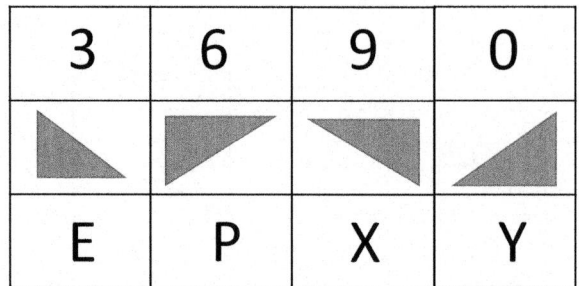

A. 9 0 P ◣   B. ◥ 3 0 9   C. ◣ 6 9 ◢   D. ◣ 6 X ◣

Question 6

Which of the answers below is an alternative to the code **7F8 ↑** ?

A. 9↓WK   B. T5KW   C. 57←W   D. 9587

Question 7

Which of the answers below is an alternative to the code **Y96R**?

F	Y	I	♥
R	◯	0	9
1	4	◖	6

A. 4691   B. 1◖◯9   C. I♥◖9   D. F◯I♥

Question 8

Which of the answers below is an alternative to the code **5DA**?

R	A	F	S
1	3	5	7
D	◄	B	➤

A. DF3   B. 5S1   C. F1◄   D. 5D➤

Question 9

Which of the answers below is an alternative to the code **GMN**?

T	G	⌐	5
2	○	N	M
⊘	9	0	F
7	8	X	✤

A. 9N2   B. ○F2   C. 9✤X   D. M9N

Question 10

Which of the answers below is an alternative to the code **PON**?

▶	H	O	5
F	↑	T	N
8	P	0	✖
4	★	X	1

A. HX1   B. ↑O▶   C. ▶↑O   D. 1▶O

ANSWERS TO WORK RATE TEST (PART 1)

Q1. D

Q2. B

Q3. C

Q4. D

Q5. B

Q6. B

Q7. A

Q8. C

Q9. C

Q10. A

PART 2 OF WORK RATE

You have 10 minutes to complete the 10 questions.

Question 1

Which of the answers below is an alternative to the code **281**?

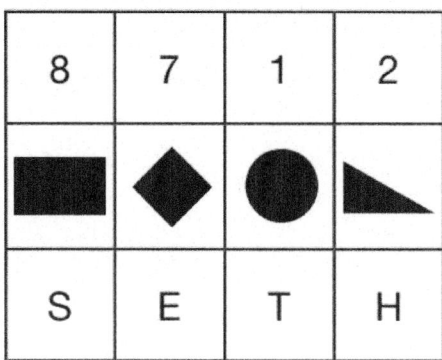

A. 8▬E   B. HS●   C. ◣5◆   D. T▬H

[ ]

Question 2

Which of the answers below is an alternative to the code **493**?

4	2	9	3
◆	▬	◣	●
D	A	Q	X

A. D◣X   B. ◆QA   C. ◣AD   D. DAX

[ ]

Question 3

Which of the answers below is an alternative to the code **987**?

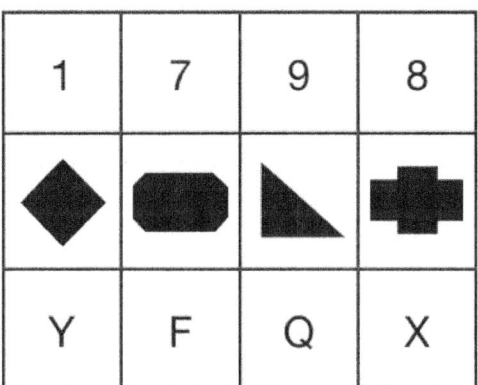

A. F▲Y   B. ◆XY   C. ✜Y◆   D. QX⬭

Question 4

Which of the answers below is an alternative to the code **135**?

A. A▲X   B. ▲AN   C. ➡XL   D. ➡LX

Question 5

Which of the answers below is an alternative to the code **1WR**?

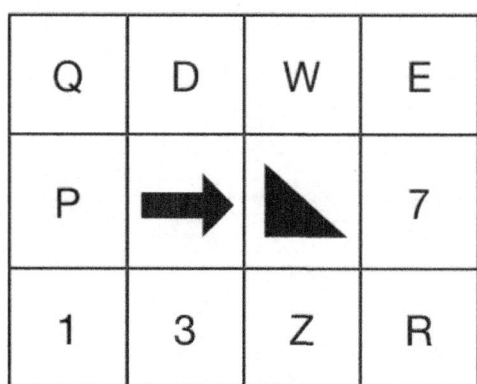

A. PZE **B.** ▲ 17 **C.** ➡1R **D.** Q3R

Question 6

Which of the answers below is an alternative to the code **DAE**?

A. Q17 **B.** Q6 **C.** ⬅16 **D.** ERA

Question 7

Which of the answers below is an alternative to the code **326**?

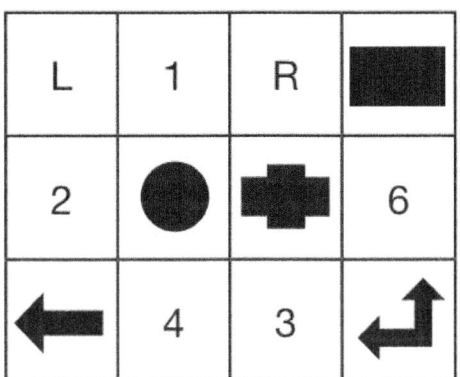

A. RL ⤴ **B.** ⤴21 **C.** ✚L4 **D.** R62

Question 8

Which of the answers below is an alternative to the code **£4&**?

L	1	R	£
2	9	&	6
=	4	3	>

A. 61> **B.** >9= **C.** >1R **D.** =13

Question 9

Which of the answers below is an alternative to the code **Q3%**?

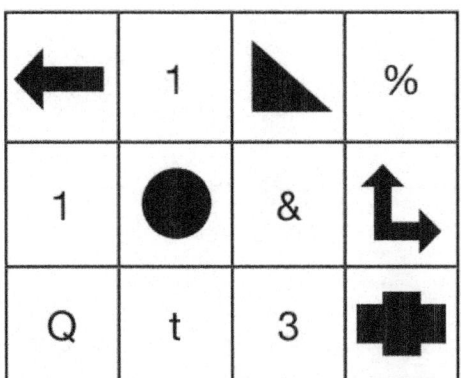

A. 1& ↰ B. 13& C. t✚1 D. 11&

Question 10

Which of the answers below is an alternative to the code **1>6**?

A. +d< B. d+< C. ✚d< D. 1>%

ANSWERS TO WORK RATE TEST (PART 2)

Q1. B

Q2. A

Q3. D

Q4. C

Q5. A

Q6. C

Q7. A

Q8. C

Q9. A

Q10. B

Now that you've completed sample questions for work rate, let's take a look at the next section – mechanical comprehension.

CHAPTER 7 – MECHANICAL COMPREHENSION

RAF DEFENCE APTITUDE ASSESSMENT

During the Royal Air Force Defence Aptitude Assessment, you will be required to sit a Mechanical Comprehension Test.

Mechanical Comprehension Tests are an assessment that measures an individual's ability to learn and understand mechanical concepts.

During the actual Mechanical Comprehension Test with the RAF, you will have a specific amount of time to answer each question. Read the questions carefully and then choose the correct answer.

In the real test, there are 20 questions you need to answer. You will be given 10 minutes to complete this assessment.

CHAPTER 7 – MECHANICAL COMPREHENSION

Question 1

A block and tackle refers to a device which is used to:

A. Place under the wheel of a car to stop it from rolling backwards.

B. Catch large fish.

C. Leverage a stationary object.

D. Hoist an object upwards by means of rope and pulleys.

Question 2

Which man is carrying less weight?

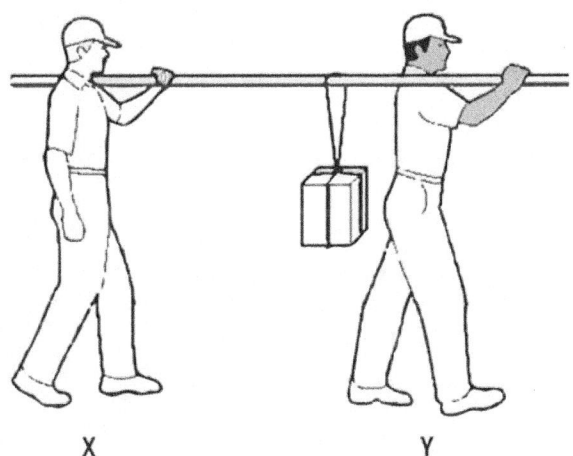

A. Man X

B. Man Y

Question 3

If wheel A rotates clockwise, which of the other wheels will also rotate clockwise?

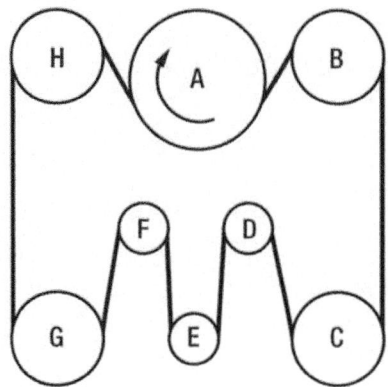

A. All of them

B. B, C, E, G and H

C. D and F

D. D, E and F

Question 4

A builder is told to pitch his ladder a third of the working height away from the building below. How many metres away from the building should the foot of the ladder be placed?

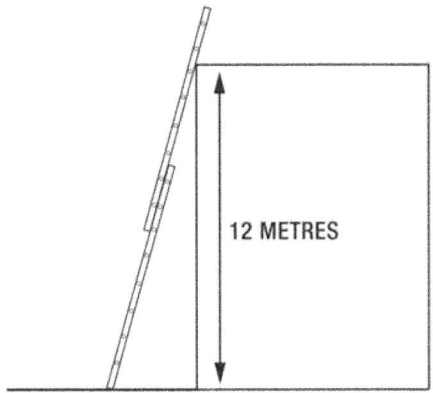

A	B	C	D
36 metres	12 metres	4 metres	3 metres

Question 5

If the object on the left side of the scale is 32 ft. away from the balance point, i.e. the fulcrum, and a force is applied 8 ft. from the fulcrum on the right side, what is the mechanical advantage?

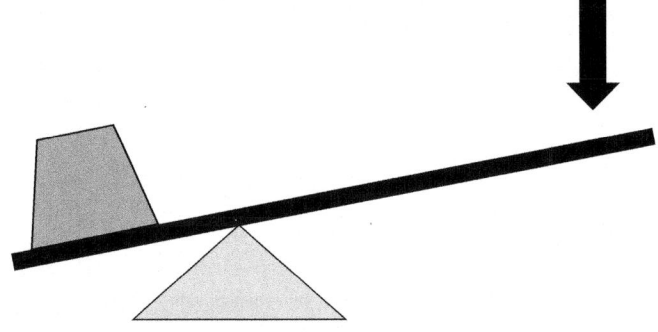

A	B	C	D
4	4.5	18	36

Question 6

A hot air balloon is able to float because:

A. The hot air is turbo-charged

B. The hot air is less dense than the external air

C. The hot air is denser than the external air

D. It is filled with helium

Question 7

Which of the following materials will float on water?

A	B	C	D
Balsa Wood	Concrete	Coins	Anchor

Question 8

Water is flowing into the following tank through the left-hand side inlet pipe at a rate of 18 litres per minute. If the water is flowing out through the lower right-hand side outlet pipe at a rate of 14 litres per minute, approximately how much time will it take for the tank to overflow?

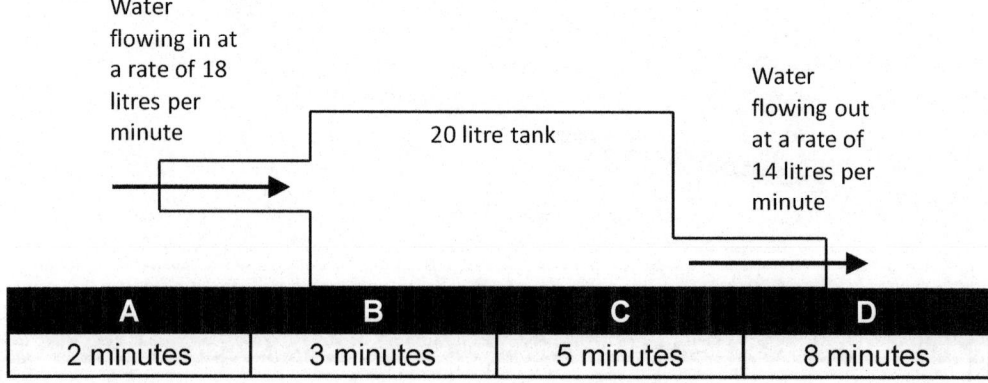

A	B	C	D
2 minutes	3 minutes	5 minutes	8 minutes

Question 9

How much weight will need to be placed on the right-hand side to balance the beam?

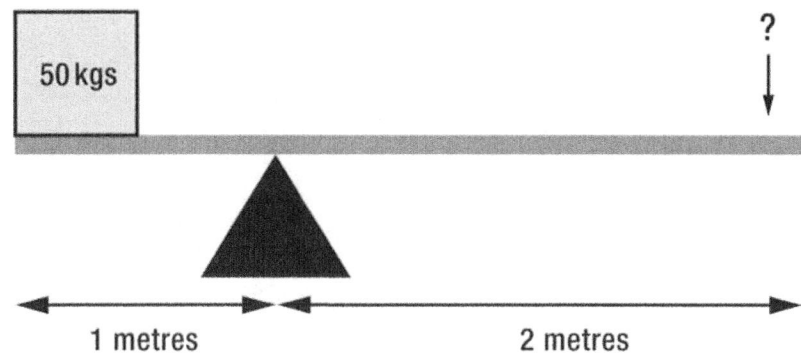

A	B	C	D
100 kgs	200 kgs	50 kgs	25 kgs

Question 10

If the wheel rotates anticlockwise, what will happen to X?

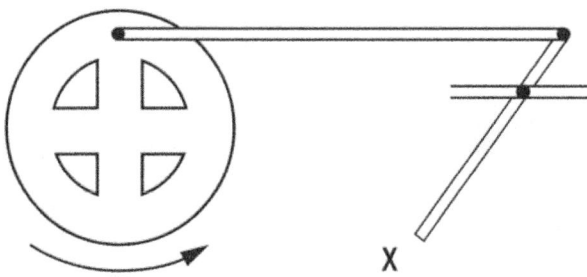

A. It will move to the right and stop.

B. It will move to the left and stop.

C. It will move left and right.

Question 11

Which chain will support the load on its own?

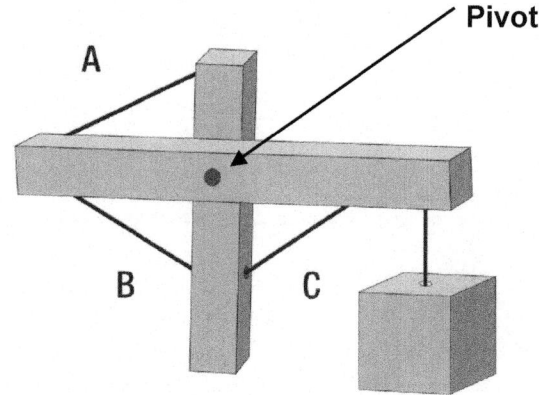

A	B	C	D
Chain A	Chain B	Chain C	None of them

Question 12

Which nail is likely to pull out first?

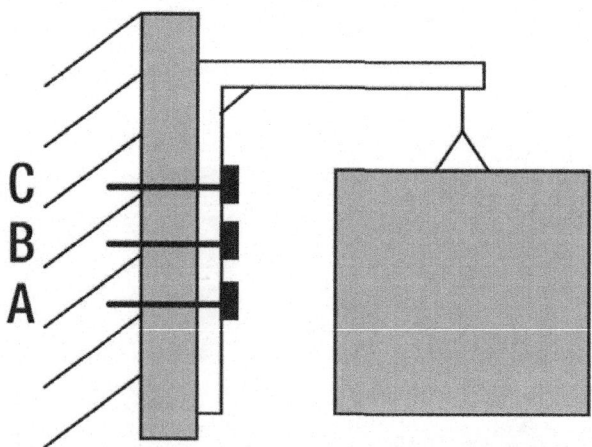

A	B	C	D
Nail A	Nail B	Nail C	All together

Question 13

If wheel A rotates anti-clockwise, which way, and how, will wheel B rotate?

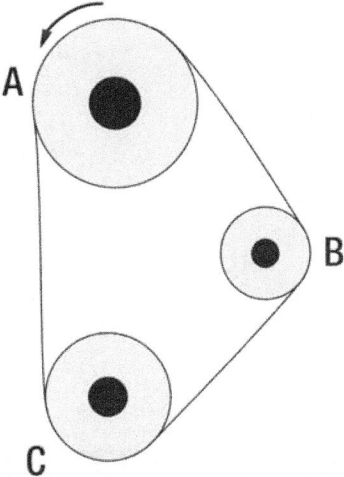

A	B	C	D
Clockwise / more rps	Clockwise / less rps	Anti-clockwise / more rps	Anti-clockwise / less rps

Question 14

Which way, and how, will cog C rotate?

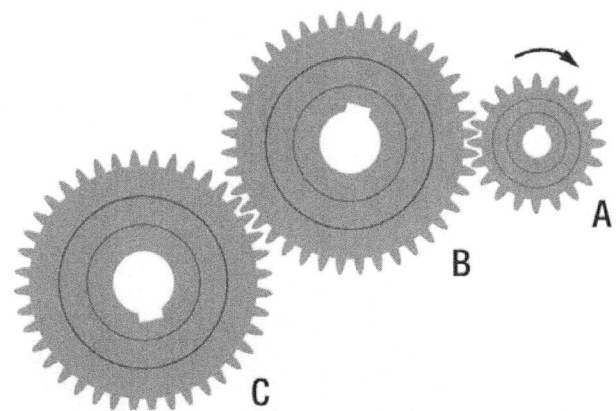

A	B	C	D
Clockwise / more rps than A	Clockwise / less rps than A	Anti-clockwise / more rps than A	Anti-clockwise / less rps than A

Question 15

Which lever will require more effort to lift the load?

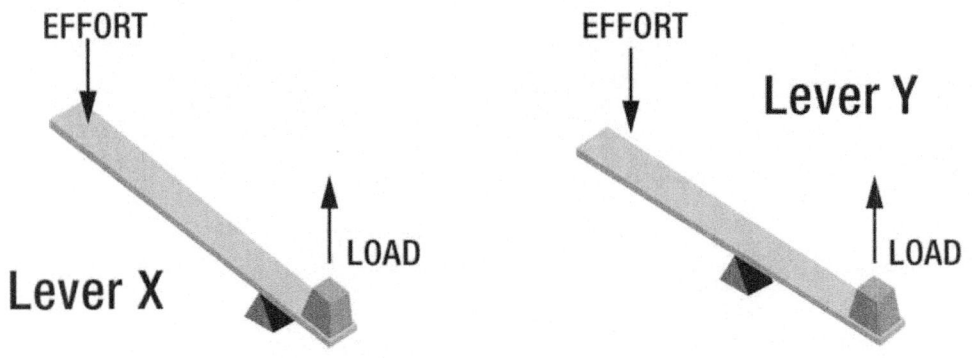

A	B	C
Lever X	Lever Y	Both the same

Question 16

How much force is required to lift the load?

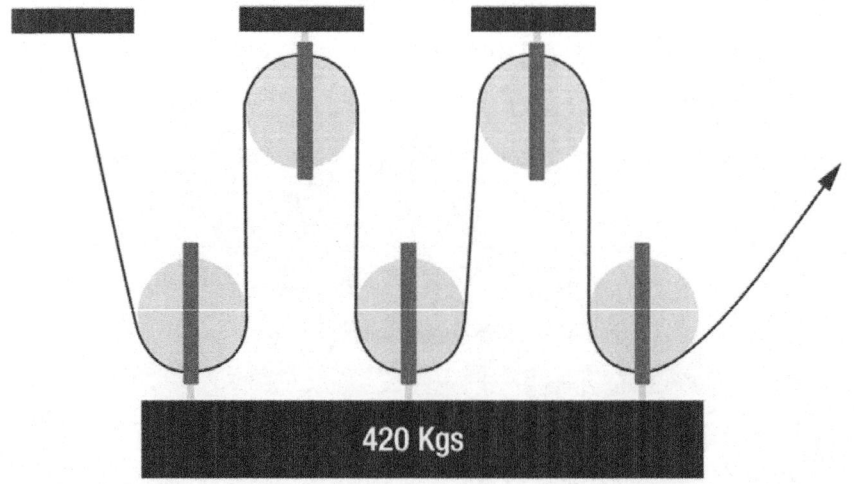

A	B	C	D
140 kgs	210 kgs	90 kgs	70 kgs

Question 17

How much weight is required to hold the load?

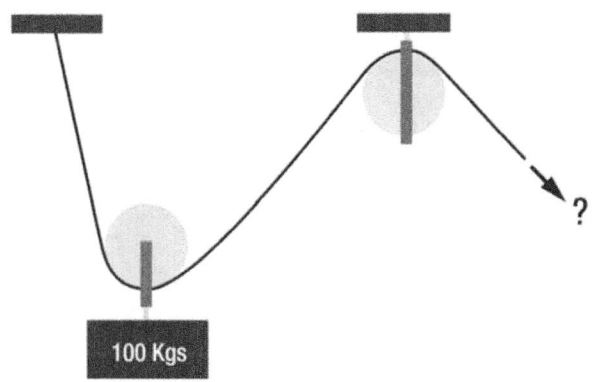

A	B	C	D
400 kgs	200 kgs	100 kgs	50 kg

Question 18

If lever A moves in the direction shown, which way will B move?

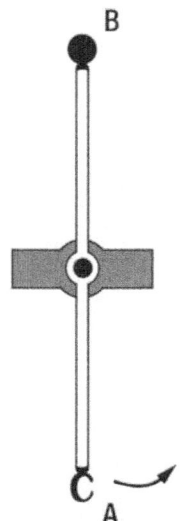

A	B	C	D
To the left	To the right	Backwards and forwards	It will not move

Question 19

If the motor wheel rotates in a clockwise direction, what happens to B and C?

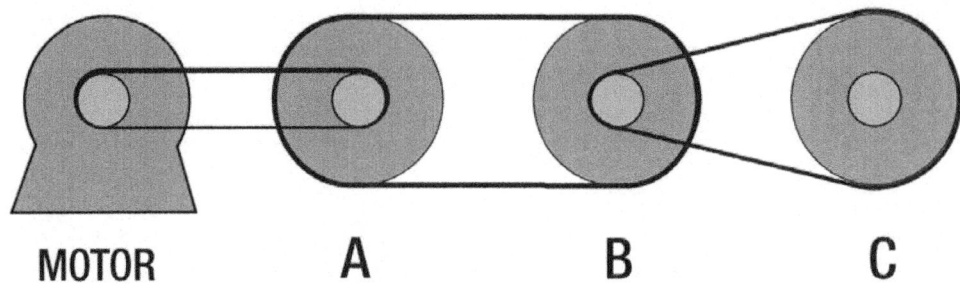

A. B and C will move clockwise.

B. B and C will move anti-clockwise.

C. B will move clockwise, and C will move anti-clockwise.

D. B will move anti-clockwise, and C will move clockwise.

Question 20

If weight is placed on the top of each stack of boxes, which stack would support the most weight?

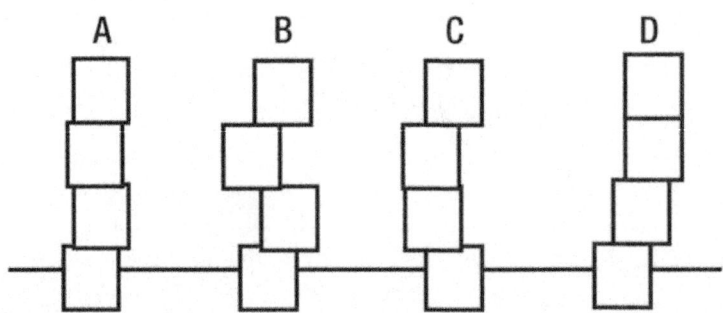

A	B	C	D
Stack A	Stack B	Stack C	Stack D

CHAPTER 7 – MECHANICAL COMPREHENSION   127

ANSWERS TO MECHANICAL COMPREHENSION TEST 1

Q1. d

A block and tackle is used to hoist an object upwards by means of rope and pulleys

Q2. A = x

You will see that the object is closer to man Y than man X. Therefore, man X is carrying less weight.

Q3. c

Wheel F and D are the only other wheels which will rotate clockwise.

Q4. c

The working height is 12 metres. The foot of the ladder must be placed 4 metres away from the building. (12 ÷ 3 = 4)

Q5. a

The effort force where the weight is to be applied (where the arrow is pointing) is equal to the resistance weight of the object on the left side of the scales. To work out the mechanical advantage, you can use the following formula: divide the length of the effort by the length of the resistance. So, 32 ÷ 8 = 4. Thus, the mechanical advantage is 4.

Q6. b

The hot air inside a hot air balloon is less dense than the external air.

Q7. a

Balsa wood is the only material here that will float on water.

Q8. c

Water is flowing in at a rate of 18 litres per minute; however, because water is also leaving the tank at a rate of 14 litres per minute, this means that only 4 litres per minute is effectively filling the tank. If the tank has a capacity of 20 litres, then it will take 5 minutes for it to overflow.

Q9. d

In order to calculate the weight required in this type of situation you can make use of the following formula:

- f = (w x d1) ÷ d2
- f = force required w = weight
- d1 = distance 1 d2 = distance 2
- f = (50 x 1) ÷ 2
- (50 ÷ 2 = 25 kg)

Q10. c

It will move left and right as the wheel rotates.

Q11. b

Chain B is the only one which can support the load independently.

Q12. c

Nail C is most likely to pull out first.

Q13. c

Wheel B will rotate anti-clockwise with more rps because it is smaller than the other two wheels.

Q14. b

Cog C will rotate clockwise with less rps than A because it has more teeth.

Q15. b

Lever Y will require more effort to lift the load because the fulcrum is further away from the load than lever X.

Q16. d

The load weighs 420 kgs and there are a total of six sections of rope supporting it. In order to calculate the force required to lift the load, simply divide the weight by the number of ropes in order to reach your answer:

- 420 ÷ 6 = 70 kg

CHAPTER 7 – MECHANICAL COMPREHENSION

Q17. d

In this scenario the weight is suspended by two pulleys. This means the weight is split equally between the two pulleys. If you want to hold the weight you only have to apply half the weight of the load, i.e. 100 ÷ 2 = 50 kgs.

Q18. a

B will move to the left in this situation.

Q19. a

B and C will move clockwise as the motor wheel moves clockwise.

Q20. a

Stack A is the most stable and will therefore support the most weight.

130 RAF DEFENCE APTITUDE ASSESSMENT

Question 1

If wheel A turns in an anti-clockwise direction, which way will wheel B turn?

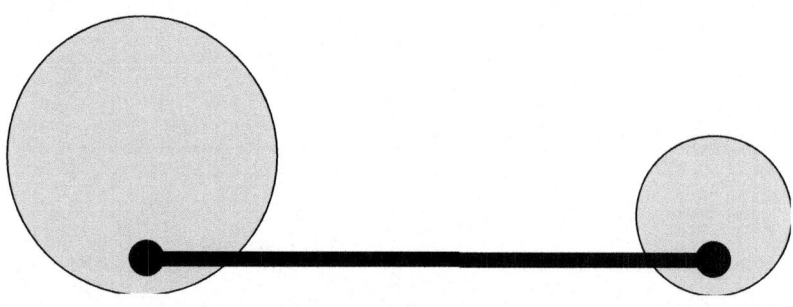

A	B	C	D
Clockwise	Anti-clockwise	Backwards and forwards	It won't move

Question 2

Which post is carrying the lightest load?

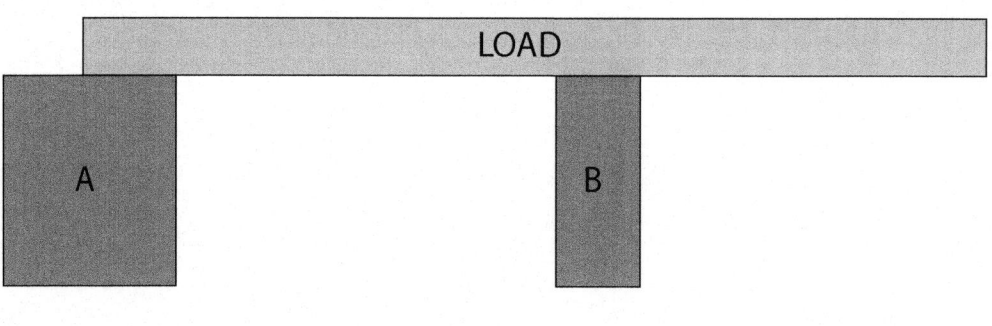

A. Post A

B. Post B

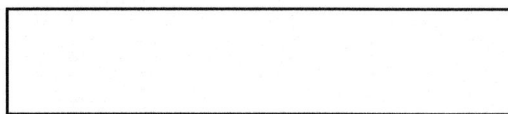

Question 3

Which pendulum will swing at the fastest speed rate?

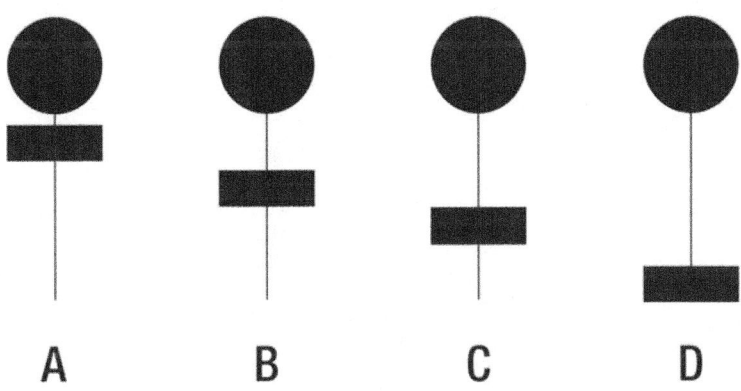

A	B	C	D
Pendulum A	Pendulum B	Pendulum C	Pendulum D

Question 4

If Cog B turns clockwise, which of the other cogs will also turn clockwise?

A	B	C	D
Cogs D and C	Cogs A, C and E	Cog D	Cogs D and E

Question 5

If Cog A moves in a clockwise direction, which way will Cog B turn?

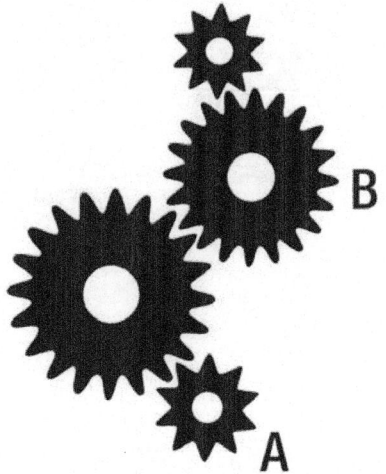

A. Clockwise

B. Anti-clockwise

Question 6

Which shelf will break first when a heavy load is placed on the whole shelf?

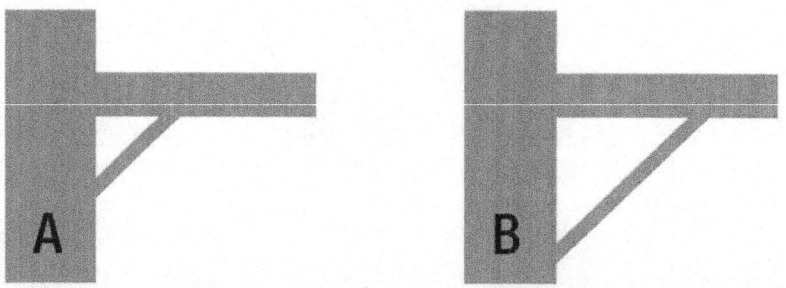

A	B	C
Shelf A	Shelf B	Both the same

CHAPTER 7 – MECHANICAL COMPREHENSION

Question 7

At which point will the pendulum be travelling at the fastest speed?

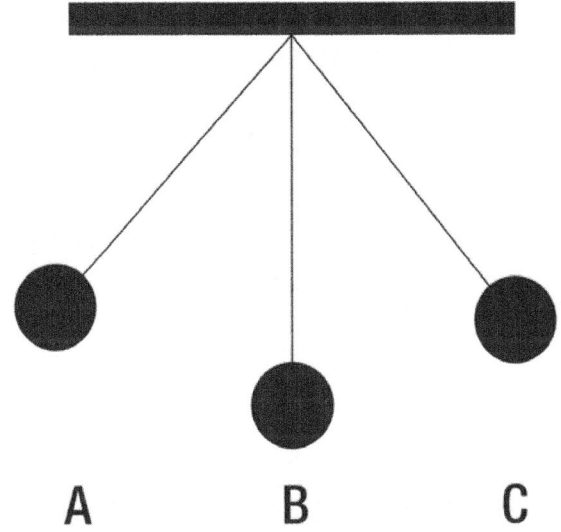

A	B	C
Point A and C	Point B	Point C

Question 8

At which point will the beam balance?

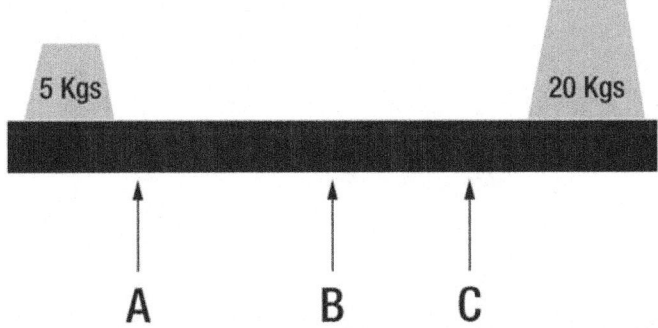

A	B	C
Point A	Point B	Point C

Question 9

If water is poured into the narrow tube, up to point 'X', what height would it reach in the wide tube?

A	B	C
Point A	Point B	Point C

Question 10

Ball X and Ball Y are both made from the same material. At which point would Ball Y have to be placed to balance Ball X?

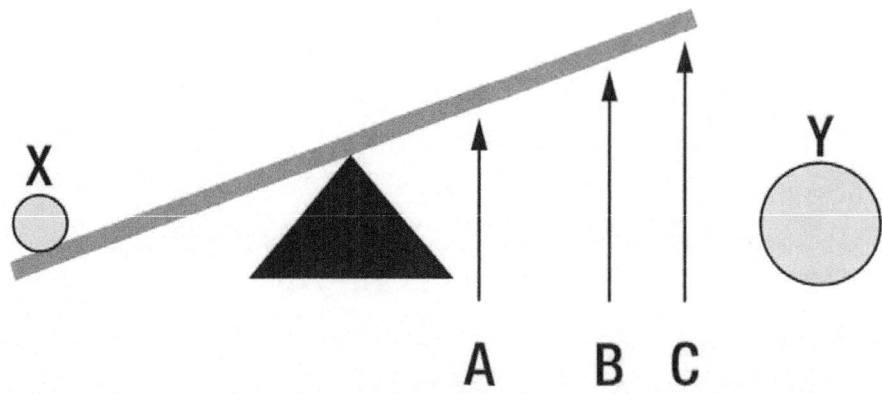

A	B	C
Point A	Point B	Point C

CHAPTER 7 – MECHANICAL COMPREHENSION

Question 11

If Cog F rotates clockwise, which way will Cog A turn?

A	B	C
Cannot say	Clockwise	Anti-clockwise

Question 12

What is the mechanical advantage?

A	B	C	D
1	2	3	4

Question 13

If water is poured in at Point D, which tube will overflow first?

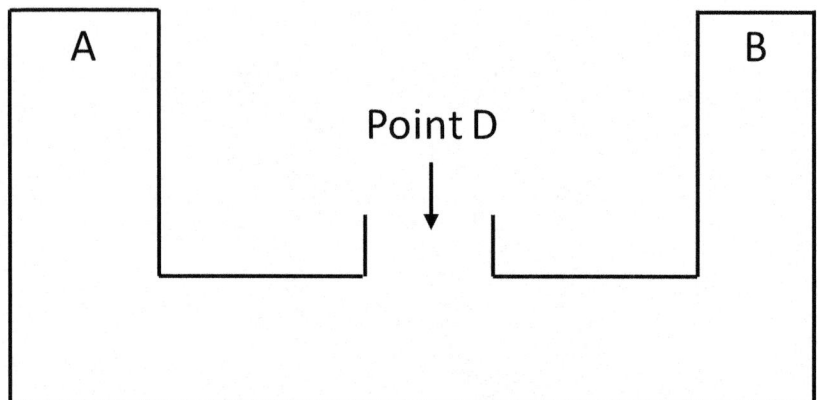

A	B	C
Tube A	Both the same	Tube B

Question 14

What is the mechanical advantage?

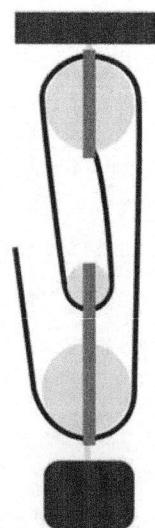

A	B	C	D
1	2	3	4

Question 15

If rope A is pulled in the direction of the arrow, which way will wheel C turn?

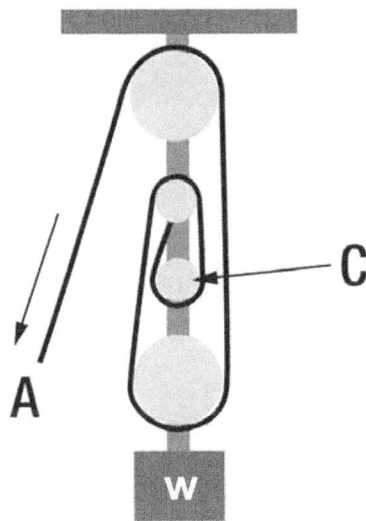

A	B	C
Clockwise	Anti-clockwise	It will not turn

Question 16

Which load is the heaviest?

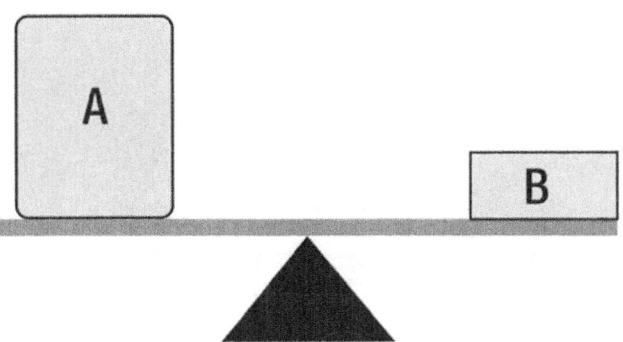

A	B	C
Both the same	Load B	Load A

Question 17

Which pulley system is a moveable pulley system?

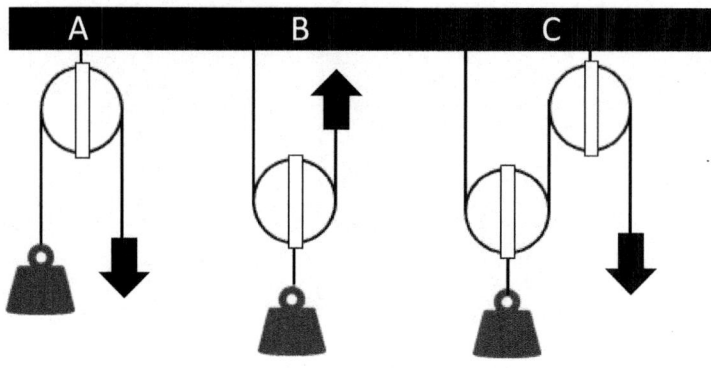

A	B	C
Pulley A	Pulley B	Pulley C

Question 18

If cog A turns anticlockwise at a speed of 20 rpm (revolutions per minute), how will cog B turn?

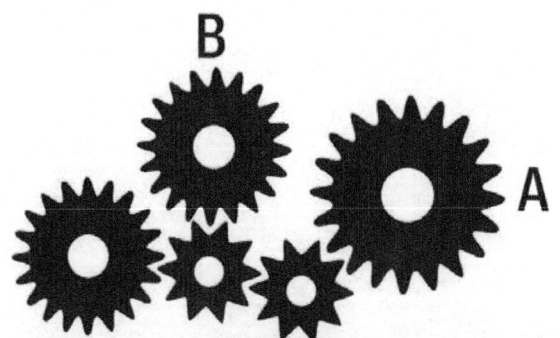

A	B	C	D
Clockwise, 20 rpm	Anti-clockwise, 20 rpm	Clockwise, 10 rpm	Anti-clockwise, 10 rpm

CHAPTER 7 – MECHANICAL COMPREHENSION

Question 19

Which pulley system will be the easiest to lift the bucket of water?

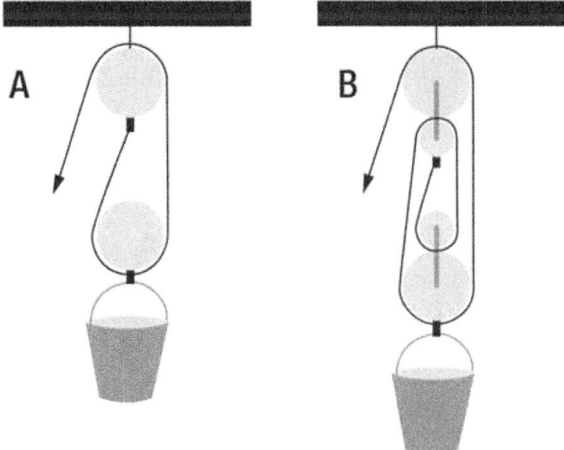

A	B	C
Both the same	Pulley A	Pulley B

Question 20

Ball A and B are an identical size and weight. If they are both released at the same time, what will happen?

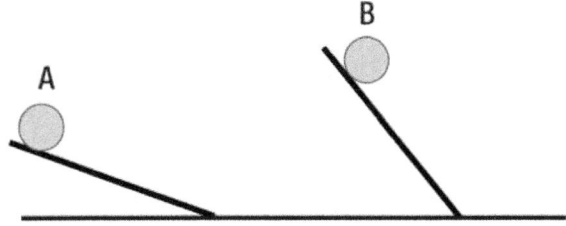

A. Ball A will reach the ground first.

B. Ball B will reach the ground first.

C. They will both reach the ground at the same time.

ANSWERS TO MECHANICAL COMPREHENSION TEST 2

Q1. b

Because the two wheels are joined they will rotate the same way. If A rotates anticlockwise, wheel B will also.

Q2. a

Post A is carrying the least heavy load as the majority of force is placed on post B.

Q3. a

Pendulum A will swing the fastest speed rate. The lower down the weight, the slower the pendulum will swing.

Q4. c

Cog D is the only other cog which will rotate clockwise.

Q5. a

Cog B will rotate clockwise.

Q6. a

Shelf A will break first, simply because the supporting bar is at a shallower angle than B.

Q7. b

Point B will be the fastest speed. At points A and C the pendulum will be reaching, or have reached, its maximum velocity before falling back down.

Q8. c

In order to balance the beam the point of balance will move closer to the heavier weight. In this case the 20 Kg weight.

Q9. b

The water will rise to the same level on the opposite side as point X.

CHAPTER 7 – MECHANICAL COMPREHENSION

Q10. a

In order to balance the beam Ball Y will need to be placed closer to the fulcrum point.

Q11. b

Cog A will rotate clockwise.

Q12. c

The mechanical advantage of this pulley system is 3. There are three supporting ropes.

Q13. b

Both entrance and exit points of the container are level, therefore, both will overflow at the same time.

Q14. d

The mechanical advantage of this pulley system is 4. There are four supporting ropes.

Q15. b

Wheel C will rotate anti-clockwise if rope A is pulled in the direction shown.

Q16. a

Both loads are of equal weight. Do not fall in to the trap of thinking load A is heavier simply because it looks larger. The key to answering this question is to look at the balancing bar. You will see that in this case it is level, meaning that both loads weigh the same.

Q17. b

Pulley system B is a moveable pulley system.

Q18. a

Cog B will turn clockwise at a speed of 20 rpm.

Q19. c

Pulley B will be the easiest to lift the load. Pulley A has a mechanical advantage of 2 whereas pulley B has a mechanical advantage of 4.

Q20. b

Although the distance each ball has to travel is identical, ball B will hit the ground first because the incline is steeper.

CHAPTER 8 — ELECTRICAL COMPREHENSION

During the DAA, you will be required to sit an Electrical Comprehension Test.

The test itself is designed to assess your ability to work with different electrical concepts.

During the actual Electrical Comprehension Test with the RAF, you will have a specific amount of time to answer each question. Read the questions carefully and then choose the correct answer.

In the real test, there are 21 questions you need to answer. You will be given 11 minutes to complete this assessment.

CHAPTER 8 – ELECTRICAL COMPREHENSION

ELECTRICAL COMPREHENSION TEST

You have 11 minutes to complete the 21 questions.

Question 1

In the following circuit, if switch A closes, and switch B remains open, what will happen?

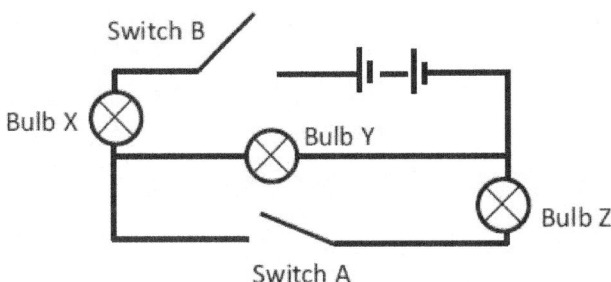

A = Bulbs X, Y, and Z will illuminate.

B = Bulb X will illuminate only.

C = Bulbs Y and Z will illuminate.

D = No bulbs will illuminate.

Question 2

A bicycle uses a battery operated light for its front and rear lights. The front and rear lights are often of different sized bulbs. The filament in the rear lamp has a resistance of 4 ohms. It takes a current of 0.3A. What voltage does the lamp work at?

A	B	C	D
1.8V	0.075V	0.7V	1.2V

Question 3

What will be the voltage at point A, if the battery is 12 volts?

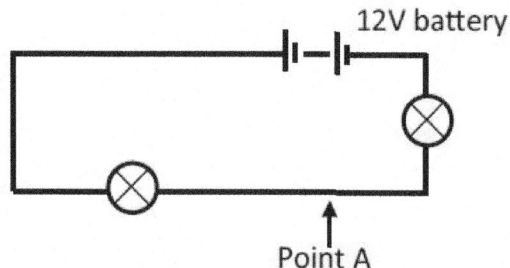

A	B	C	D
0 volts	3 volts	12 volts	6 volts

Question 4

An atom's atomic number is determined by the number of what?

A	B	C	D
Neutrons	Protons	Electrons	Atoms

Question 5

In the following electrical circuit, if switch B closes, what will happen?

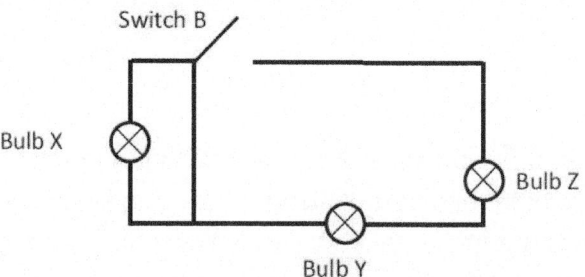

A	B	C	D
Bulbs X, Y and Z will illuminate	Bulb X will illuminate	Bulbs Y and Z will illuminate	No bulbs will illuminate

Question 6

Ammeters measure the amount of current in a circuit. In the circuit below, all of the ammeters are identical. If ammeter A1 reads 0.8A, what will ammeter A3 read?

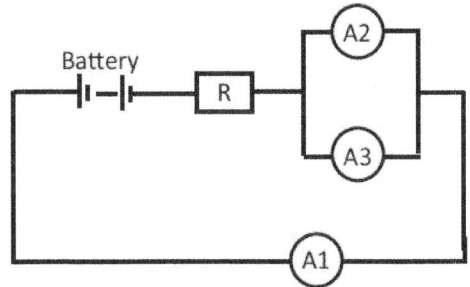

A	B	C	D
0.12A	0.8A	0.4A	0.24A

Question 7

What happens when an electrical charge flows through a resistor?

A = The temperature decreases.

B = The temperature increases.

C = The temperature fluctuates.

D = The temperature stays the same.

Question 8

What is the current in the circuit below?

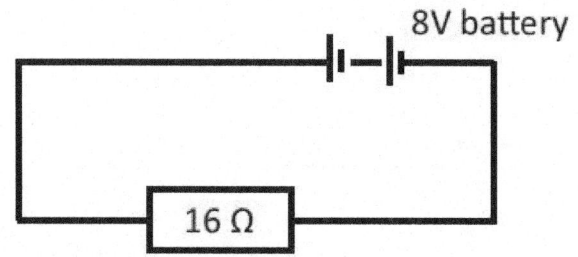

A	B	C	D
2A	1.2A	0.5A	8A

Question 9

Insert the two missing words:

Voltage is a measure of the difference in _____ _____ between two parts of a circuit. The bigger the difference in energy, the bigger the voltage.

A = Electrical current

B = Flowing amperes

C = Concurrent electricity

D = Electrical energy

Question 10

In the following circuit, how many bulbs will illuminate if switches 1 and 5 close?

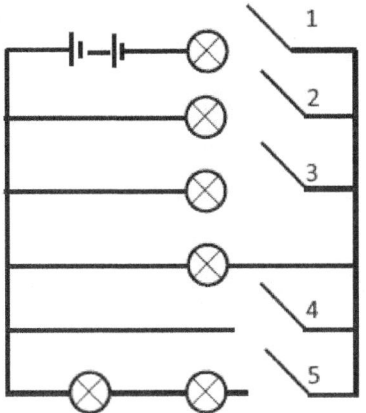

A	B	C	D
2	3	4	5

Question 11

Insert the two missing words:

At a low temperature, the resistance of a thermistor _____ is and allows for _____ current to flow through.

A = High, little.

B = Low, little.

C = High, more.

D = Low, more.

Question 12

Computer monitors and television screens are often covered in dust because...

A = The dust is attracted by the cool air of the technological device.

B = Dust is unmanageable.

C = The dust is attracted to the microfibres of the screen.

D = The dust is attracted by the static charges compelling from the technological device.

Question 13

What is the voltage across the battery?

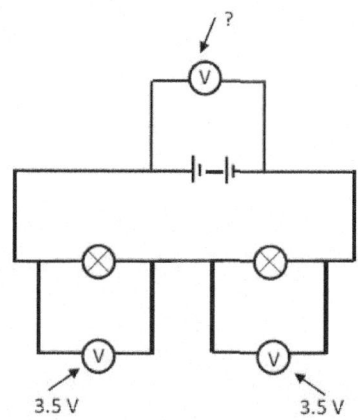

A	B	C	D
3.5V	12.25V	7V	1.25V

Question 14

Insert the two missing words:

Current is a measure of how much _____ _____ flows through a circuit. The more charge that flows, the bigger the current.

A = Electrical energy.

B = Electrical current.

C = Flowing amperes.

D = Electrical charge.

Question 15

Which of these diagrams of the ammeters is connected correctly?

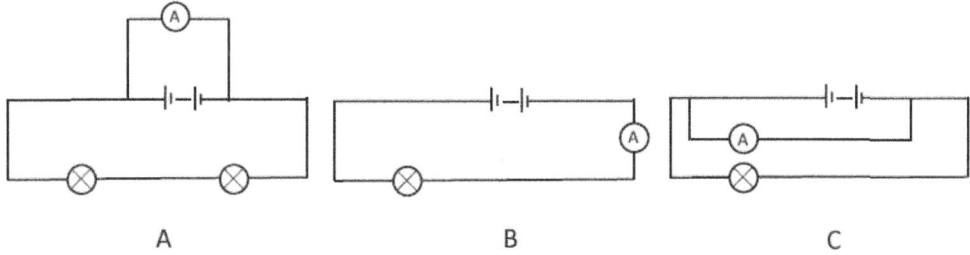

A	B	C
Diagram A	Diagram B	Diagram C

Question 16

In the circuit below, if one bulb blows, what would happen to the other bulbs in the circuit?

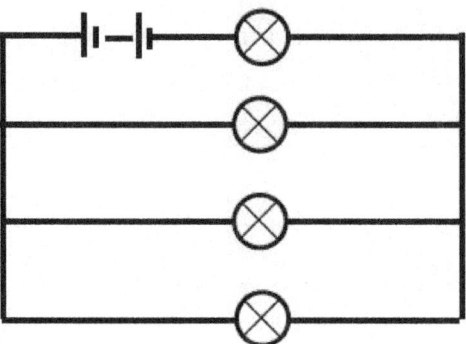

A	B	C	D
Stay lit, but dims	Stay lit, with same brightness	Stay lit, and brightens	No bulbs will illuminate

Question 17

Which of the following statements is true in relation to parallel circuits?

A = The resistance is shared between each of the components connected in parallel of the circuit.

B = The voltage is shared between each of the components connected in parallel of the circuit.

C = The current is shared between each of the components connected in parallel of the circuit.

D = None of the above.

CHAPTER 8 – ELECTRICAL COMPREHENSION

Question 18

Electrical potential difference also means _____.

A = Current

B = Resistance

C = Voltage

D = Parallel circuit

Question 19

What does a transformer do to electrical currents?

A = Changes the voltage.

B = It turns electricity into power.

C = It adds more watts.

D = It conducts heat from the transformer component.

Question 20

Which electrical component is the following a description of?

A safety device which will blow, i.e. 'melt', if the current through it exceeds a specified value.

A	B	C	D
Battery	Fuse	Switch	Resistor

Question 21

When an aeroplane is being refuelled, to avoid causing a spark which could build up from static charge...

A = The person pouring in the fuel needs to pour it in slowly.

B = The aeroplane has rubber tyres which insulates the charges.

C = The refuelling tank and the aeroplane itself are earthed.

D = The person pouring in the fuel needs to pour it in fast.

E = The person needs to be electronically uncharged.

ANSWERS TO ELECTRICAL COMPREHENSION TEST

Q1. D = no bulbs will illuminate

- If switch A closes, and switch B remains open, no bulbs will illuminate. Even with switch A being an 'on-switch', the fact that switch B remains open means that the power supply (i.e. the battery) cannot supply the power because the circuit is broken.

Q2. D = 1.2V

- In order to work out the voltage, you need to multiply the resistance by the current. So, 4 × 0.3 = 1.2V.

Q3. C = 12 volts

- In a series circuit, there is only one path for the current, and therefore that current is the same at all points of the path.

Q4. B = protons

- An atomic number is determined by the number of protons in an atom's nucleus.

Q5. D = no bulbs will illuminate

- The reason that no bulbs will illuminate is because, and although the switch would become an 'on-switch', there is no power source to generate anything, and therefore the bulbs would not be lit.

Q6. C = 0.4A

- If ammeter A1 reads 0.8, then ammeters A2 and A3 will have to share this current, therefore each of these would read 0.4.

Q7. B = the temperature increases

- When an electrical charge flows through a resistor, the temperature increases. The resistor gets hot from the electrical charge running through it, therefore increasing the temperature.

Q8. C = 0.5A

- The current in this circuit is as follows: $8 \div 16 = 0.5A$.

Q9. D = electrical energy

- The two words that are missing in the sentence are 'electrical energy'. Voltage is a measure of the difference in electrical energy between two parts of a circuit.

Q10. C = 4

- If switches 1 and 5 were closed, 4 bulbs would illuminate. The bulb left of switch 1 would illuminate, the two bulbs left of switch 5 would illuminate, and the bulb on the fourth horizontal line would illuminate.

Q11. A = high, little

- At a low temperature, the resistance of a thermistor is high, and little current can flow through. In comparison, at a high temperature, the resistance of a thermistor is low, and allows for more current to flow through.

Q12. D = the dust is attracted by the static charges compelling from the technological device

- Computer screens and television screens are often covered in dust because the dust becomes attracted by the static charges compelling from the technological device. The electrical element of statics can be demonstrated when two objects rub together and become 'electronically charged'. When you remove the dust, you often hear the static electricity 'snapping'.

Q13. C = 7V

- The circuit contains two elements that share the voltage. Therefore, the overall voltage of the battery is as follows: 3.5 + 3.5 = 7V.

Q14. D = electrical charge

- In order for the sentence to make sense, the two words that you would need to enter into the sentence are 'electrical charge'. So, the sentence would read 'current is a measure of how much electrical charge flows through a circuit. The more charge that flows, the bigger the current'.

Q15. B = diagram B

- Diagram B is wired correctly because ammeters need to be wired in a series circuit. The ammeter needs to be connected by one path of wiring.

Q16. B = stay lit, with same brightness

- If one of the bulbs goes out, it does not affect the other bulbs. The bulbs are all placed on different paths which are linked by the same battery. Therefore, if one path stops working, the others will continue to work. This does not affect the brightness of the bulbs as the bulbs are still powered by the same amount of power from the battery.

Q17. C = the current is shared between each of the components connected in parallel of the circuit.

- Within a parallel circuit, the current is shared amongst each component that is connected in parallel.

Q18. C = voltage

- Electrical potential difference is also the same as voltage. Voltage can be defined as measuring the difference in electrical energy.

Q19. A = changes the voltage

- A transformer component within an electrical circuit is a device whereby it transfers energy between two or more circuits. With an alternating current, a transformer will increase or decrease the voltage as it makes the transfer.

Q20. B = fuse

- A fuse can be used as a safety device which will blow, i.e. melt, if the current through it exceeds a specified value. A fuse consists of a strip of wire that melts/breaks an electrical circuit when the current is deemed to be at an unsafe level.

Q21. C = the refuelling tank and the aeroplane itself are earthed

- When a tank of an aeroplane is being refuelled, the refuelling tank and the aeroplane are earthed. A bonding line is used to earth the aeroplane before it is refuelled, in order to ensure that it is safe to add fuel to the aircraft's tank.

Now that you've completed sample questions for electrical comprehension, let's take a look at the final section – memory tests.

CHECK OUT OUR RAF RANGE OF RESOURCES!

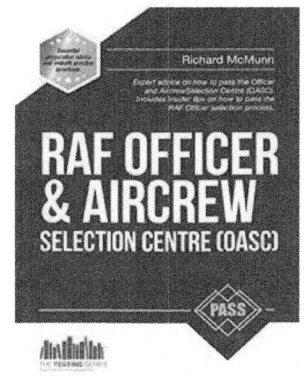

How2Become have created these other FANTASTIC guides to aid you through every career for the RAF.

FOR MORE INFORMATION ON OUR RAF GUIDES, PLEASE CHECK OUT THE FOLLOWING:

WWW.HOW2BECOME.COM

ROYAL AIR FORCE COURSE

- Online masterclass - immediate access.
- Learn how to pass each stage of the RAF selection process.
- The course will cover the application form, the assessment centre and the interview.

WWW.HOW2BECOME.COM

Get Access To
FREE
RAF Resources

www.How2Become.com

 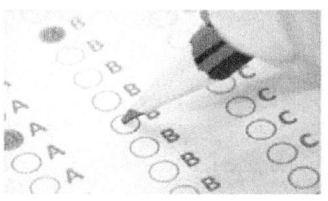 

Printed in Great Britain
by Amazon